Presentation of the Pompidou Group

The Council of Europe's involvement in action against drug misuse and drug trafficking is carried out through the work of the Pompidou Group. Set up in 1971 as a European multidisciplinary platform for co-operation, the Group aims to combine information exchange on drug-related issues, scientific assessment and political decision making.

It seeks to put at the disposal of the member states tools to evaluate and tackle emerging problems in the social and public health field. In this respect, one of the key areas of activity of the Pompidou Group, its epidemiology working group, is oriented to collecting, analysing and synthesizing data, improving data collection methods and adding value to this information through policy-relevant analyses.

Since 1985, the Group is co-ordinating a series of *Multi-city Studies* aimed to assess, interpret and compare drug use trends in Europe, on the basis of a city network, recently expanded to include forty-two large cities. This has led the Group to focus on improving the quality and comparability of data and to develop instruments both for the monitoring of specific indicators such as *Treatment demand* and for prevalence investigations such as the standardised *Questionnaire for school surveys on drug, alcohol and tobacco habits* which was used in two Europe-wide surveys.

The opinions expressed in this publication are those of the authors and do not necessarily reflect those of the Council of Europe/Pompidou Group.

DRUG USE IN PRISON

by Richard Muscat

Pompidou Group
Group of Experts in Epidemiology of Drug Problems

Council of Europe Publishing

French edition:

L'usage de drogues en milieu carcéral

ISBN 92-871-4520-2

Council of Europe Publishing
F-67075 Strasbourg Cedex

ISBN 92-871-4521-0
© Council of Europe, December 2000
Printed in Germany

Contents

Report on drug use in prison

Country Reports

Report on drug use in prison

1. Background

The Recommendation No. (98) 7 of the Committee of Ministers of the Council of Europe to member states concerning the ethical organisational aspects of health care in prison was adopted by the Committee of Ministers on 8 April 1998. The opening gambit of this document makes the following recommendation: that the medical practice in the community and in prison should be guided by the same ethical principles.

In chapter III entitled "The organisation of health care in prison with specific reference to the management of certain common problems", section B is attributed to addiction to drugs, alcohol and medication and the following recommendations 43-49 have been made:

"The care of prisoners with alcohol and drug-related problems needs to be developed further taking into account in particular the services offered for drug addicts, as recommended by the Co-operation Group to Combat Drug Abuse and Illicit Trafficking in Drugs ("Pompidou Group"). Therefore it is necessary to offer sufficient training to medical and prison personnel, and to improve co-operation with external counselling services, in order to ensure continuing follow-up therapy on discharge to the community".

"The prison doctor should encourage prisoners to take advantage of the system of social or psychotherapeutic assistance in order to prevent the risk of abuse of drugs, medication and alcohol".

"The treatment of withdrawal symptoms of abuse of drugs, alcohol or medication in prison should be conducted along the same lines as in the community".

"If prisoners undergo a withdrawal cure, the doctor should encourage them, both while still in prison and after their release, to take all the necessary steps to avoid a relapse in to addiction".

"Detained persons should be able to consult a specialised internal or external counselor who would give them the necessary support both while they are serving their sentence and during their care after release. Such counsellors should be able to contribute to the in-service training of custodial staff".

"Where appropriate, prisoners should be allowed to carry their prescribed medication. However, medication which is dangerous if taken as an overdose should be withheld and issued to them on an individual dose-by-dose basis".

"In consultation with the competent pharmaceutical adviser, the prison doctor should prepare as necessary a comprehensive list of medicines and drugs usually prescribed in medical service. A medical prescription should remain the exclusive responsibility of the medical profession, and medicines should be distributed by authorised personnel only".

It would appear that these recommendations take into consideration that people using drugs do end up in prison but do not assume that drug taking continues while these individuals are serving their sentences. The EMCDDA 1998 report tries to evaluate the prevalence of drug use in prison amongst its member states. It is immediately apparent that such a phenomena does exist but the different methodologies used to calculate such figures do not make comparisons between countries easy to undertake. A significant problem has been with the definitions of drug users used in the various studies. Some have favoured any illicit drug use, whilst others have opted for intravenous drug users.

Furthermore, some studies have focussed on use before entry or the history of previous abuse whilst others have resorted to positive urine outcomes of inmates or information given by key persons. In addition, in most of the studies, the small number of prisons examined are not representative of the whole prison system, which makes it impossible to to extrapolate results to the whole country.

On the whole however, whichever parameter has been selected between a minimum of 5% and a maximum of 70% of prison populations across Europe are made up of people who have used drugs and continue to do so while incarcerated. The figures reported in Table 1 overleaf would appear to substantiate these findings.

Again, these figures to a significant extent refer to individuals with a previous history of drug use before being confined to prison. A minority of studies have however addressed the problem of drug use within the confines of prison and to all accounts it would appear that such a practice is to say the least not uncommon.

The European Network of Drug and HIV/AIDS Services in Prison in 1995 produced an estimate of 46.5% to be users of illegal drugs before incarceration that would in turn support some of the figures given in table 1.

On the other hand, The European Network on HIV/AIDS and Hepatitis Prevention in Prison have developed a methodology that is validated and well implemented in a number of countries in which it has been ascertained that intravenous drug use does occur in prison. Moreover, such behaviour is compounded in such settings as inmates are seen as more likely to share equipment thus posing serious health risks amongst this group.

Table 1: Percentage of drug users within prison populations throughout Europe.

Country	Proportion of drug users amongst prison populations
Austria	15-72%
Belgium	42%
Denmark	19-36%
Finland	31%
France	23-43%
Germany	5-60%
Greece	31%
Ireland	35-86%
Netherlands	14-29%
Spain	50%
Sweden	44%
England & Wales	15-68%
Scotland	18-43%

(Source EMCDDA (1999): Extended annual report on the state of the drug problems in the European Union.)

Finally, the Health in Prisons Project (HIPP) operated by WHO turned their attention to their third priority area, drug misuse, around February 1999. It would appear that they are going to make use of the principles and recommendations such as harm reduction, drug free units and substitution treatment, needle exchange and peer support put forward by the European Network of Drug and HIV/AIDS Services in Prison.

In the light of these activities and the recommendations made by the Committee of Ministers of the Council of Europe it became evident that drug use in prison seemed to be a prevailing phenomenon, yet no information is available to date on the possible effect of incarceration on drug use.

Approval by the Permanent Correspondents of the Pompidou Group for the Drug Use in Prison project was first sought in 1997. The project in its entirety was put forward by Ms. Luisa Machado Rodrigues (P-PG/Epid (98) 16 rev) and approval was given at the 40th meeting of the Permanent Correspondents (October 1997). Since that time two informal meetings of the group have taken place, one in Lisbon in July 1998, and the other at the first Project Group Meeting in the field of Epidemiology (30 November-1 December 1998). To date there have also been two working group meetings; the first took place in Paris in March 1999, a report of which was forwarded to all interested parties by Ms. Luisa Machado Rodrigues (P-PG/Epid (99) 9 E). The major outcome of that meeting was that a key list of words or guidelines be provided to each member by the co-ordinator for discussion at the second working group meeting (P-PG/Epid (99) 12 E). This meeting was held in Strasbourg in June 1999 and

9

following long but positive discussions it was agreed by the group that each member produce a summary of Drug use in Prison of their respective countries along the following guidelines (P-PG/Epid (99) 14 E). The key question to be addressed was that of: *"What impact does prison have on drug use?"*

In attempting to answer this question, each document incorporated the following elements.

1. Section 1 - basic information from the Guidelines.

2. Do inmates start or stop drug use while in prison?

3. Are there any changes in patterns of use from the point of view of switching from cannabis to heroin or vice-versa? In addition, are there any changes in frequency, quantity and volume of drugs used while in prison?

4. In the case of drug use are there any changes in the route of administration and what effects does prison have on the individual in the case of sharing equipment?

5. Does the fact that an individual has been sent to prison result in any changes in ongoing treatment?

6. Finally, is there any evidence that prison influences the individual's motivation to stop drug use?

The documents pertaining to the information outlined above were submitted during the month of September 1999. These in turn were made available to the participants of the seminar on "Drug Misusing Offenders in Prison and After Release" held in Strasbourg on 4-6 October 1999 organised by the Pompidou Group, Council of Europe.

2. Introduction

It is necessary before attempting to get to grips with answering the core questions of interest to provide some background information or context under which such information was gathered from the participating countries. In the first instance some basic information relating to the number of prisons, number of detainees and the percentage of drug users within the prison population is given in table 2, overleaf.

Table 2: Prison Statistics of Group members

Country	No. of prisons	No. of prisoners	% Drug users
Estonia	9	4 387	13%
France	187	53 000	32%
Greece	28	7 280	36%
Ireland	15	2 700	52%
Malta	1	240	47%
Netherlands	39	12 553	50%
Portugal	53	14 598	53%
Russian Federation	-		66%
Spain	-	38 365	50%
Slovak Republic	18	7 102	7%
United Kingdom	132	65 298	48%

On viewing the table it is immediately apparent that no attempt has been made to incorporate the number of detainees per 100 000 of the population. The table is rather meant to illustrate the fact that percentages seem to indicate that, with the exception of Estonia and the Slovak Republic, between one and two thirds of detainees have made use of drugs, generally prior to imprisonment.

These figures may be rather surprising at first if one were to examine how these individuals came to be incarcerated. It is widely assumed that the drug policy and the criminal justice system of the country in question plays a significant role and that with such different systems in operation in the participating countries such a close parody would not arise. In the majority of countries however, it would appear that the systems in operation try to provide an option through which a drug user may seek treatment.

Another overall source of confusion of table 2 is the failure to define the term drug user. This is no oversight as in the main the countries involved in this working group and also those of the European Union (EU) specify themselves what they refer to when using such a term, but it happens to be different in most of the countries concerned. In some it refers to occasional use whereas in others it refers to recreational use. In others it refers to problem drug use and under these circumstances it is normally associated with the use of opiates. Thus, if one is referring to drug use in general the figures for this cohort vary from between 25-70% or more, whereas the percentage of problem drug users is somewhat lower, between 20 and 50%. Moreover, the years for which these data have been obtained through surveys, drug tests or other means have not been included as they also vary accordingly from country to country. In the light of these caveats at this early stage of the proceedings it would be helpful to keep these factors in mind as well as to reflect on the urgent need to regularise this position which becomes all too evident by the close.

For example, in France the concept of possession for personal use does not exist, unlike other European countries. In France, use means consumption. The law prohibits use of any drug but if there are no signs of dealing every effort is made for the offender to be given treatment if they seek it. As such in 1997, of the 70 000 arrests made in respect of drug use, 3 368 convictions were handed down, of which only 494 (15%) were unsuspended sentences and the average duration of these were of the order of 2.4 months. There were 8 052 treatment orders, 245 community service orders and 203 educational measure orders.

With regard to the justice system in operation, in Ireland it is an offence to be in possession of a controlled substance. However, dependence on drug-related convictions as an indicator of drug use among prisoners has consistently been shown to obscure the true extent of the problem in Ireland. It has been recorded that although there was a fifty-fold increase in the number of drug-related charges initiated by the police between 1965 and 1993, this continued to be a small proportion of the overall number of indictable crimes. In 1995 only 3 730 of an estimated 100 000 indictable crimes were drug-related.

In Malta, it is a criminal offence to be in possession of any amount of a controlled substance. The judiciary though is rather strict in the way they interpret the amounts in question as to whether they are for personal use or to traffic. The courts however, in cases of personal use, are prepared to provide the opportunity for the individual to seek treatment if it so desired. This to some extent has to be qualified from the point of view that in the majority of cases, the time taken to trial sometimes exceeds months or years with the result that an individual may further offend resulting in multiple cases that complicate and sometimes preclude the path to treatment.

In the Netherlands however, it would appear that early intervention through law enforcement provides the means through which users may be brought into treatment. The chain of law enforcement provides for four phases: (1) the police phase; (2) the custody phase, (3) the adjournment phase and (4) the court session. Those individuals that are motivated to attend to their problem exit in the earlier phases so that those ending up in the final phases are the more problematic users who probably need intensive therapy. Again this system of segregation provides an opportunistic method to firstly embrace those individuals in need of treatment and secondly to divide them into specific groups related to their needs.

In Portugal, like most other European countries, a distinction is made between illicit production and trafficking of drugs and drug possession and consumption. These laws were adapted from the 1998 UN Convention in 1993. Penalties for production and trafficking are heavier than for possession or consumption.

However, most contraventions lead to imprisonment and only a minority lead to a suspended sentence if the individual agrees to voluntary treatment.

Judicial sentences for production, possession or trafficking in the Russian Federation resulted in imprisonment for a term of between 1-3 years as established in the 1926 Act. In 1986 however, the term was more in the order of ten years and in between the period of 1966 to 1993 drug related crimes had increased eight-fold. In the main however, these offenders were drug users and their crime in turn was related to obtaining the drug in question, be it petty theft or trafficking.

In Spain, as in the Netherlands, the law provides means through which an addict may benefit from prevention, health care and social integration programmes. In addition, there is in place a document "Global policy for drug-related issues in Penitentiary Administration" that provides strategies for dealing with these very issues. The prison population on 1 January 1999 stood at 38,365 of which 78.8% had been convicted for property crimes and drug trafficking. In the main, property crimes are typically drug related.

In the Slovak Republic, the laws on drug production, possession and trafficking were amended in October 1994 and are akin to the 1988 UN Convention. However, drug use in itself is not a punishable offence whereas possession results in prosecution. A total of 396 individuals were sentenced for drug law offences in 1998 of which 15 underwent some form of treatment.

Currently, in the United Kingdom, it is an offence to involve oneself in the production, possession or trafficking in illicit substances.

To summarise, estimates of the percentage of drug users in prison varies between 7% in the Slovak Republic to 66% in the Russian Federation. However, these figures are dependent on the use of the term drug users. In some countries this term refers to occasional drug use while in others it refers to problem drug use and thus comparisons of such estimates should be viewed with caution. Moreover, in France, the Netherlands, Spain and the United Kingdom, where drug use has been in the public domain for a number of years, the use of the judiciary system now appears to be a tool through which users are provided with the opportunity to enter into treatment and not prison. In the other countries such as Greece, Ireland, Malta, the Russian Federation and the Slovak Republic where drug use is a more recent phenomena, the judiciary are more likely to sentence users to periods of imprisonment which then puts the onus on the penal system to deal with drug users. In Portugal however, drug users in prison consist mainly of a specific cohort that are serving sentences for related crime and not drug law offences related to possession or consumption.

3. Initiation of drug use in prison

In order to answer the question of whether inmates stop or start using drugs in prison, most of the group supported the notion that some form of baseline needs to be established beforehand. The Netherlands has put forward a model in which three groups need to be distinguished, namely:

a.   non drug-user;
b.   non-identified drug user;
c.   identified drug user.

Within such a framework one could then determine whether the non drug-user started use in prison, the identified drug user continued drug use in prison or stopped drug use. A problem then arises with the non-identified drug user as to what proportion of the cohort can these be explained in terms of continued or discontimined drug use in prison. In theory however, it should be possible to extrapolate the answers to this question with the other information to hand. On the limited data available in the Netherlands with regard to discontinued drug use in prison, a small survey reports that 91% used drugs or alcohol before being sentenced while 68% responded in the affirmative to drug use during detention. No information was available as to the proportion of non-drug users that initiated drug use while in prison.

In a European survey (1997-98) conducted in seven countries including France, it was determined that irrespective of whether one was an intravenous drug user or not, on entry into prison drug use declined. However, consumption was always higher in the former group. The caveat that results from such data is whether one considers reduced drug use within the same population merely a frequency phenomena or does one assume a reduction in use as a decrease in the population use per se? Once again, no information was available on the numbers of inmates who initiated drug use while in prison.

Initiation into illicit drug use among prisoners has not been explored in the context of Irish prisons. No data are available on the extent to which prisoners are initiated into their first ever drug use within the Irish prison system. As will be seen in later sections, there is only evidence of initiation into new drugs of use or new routes of administration rather than any illicit drug use per se.

In the only prison in Malta, a guesstimate based on previous contact with the drug services assumes that 5% of the prison population first make use of drugs while serving their sentence. It also again assumed that these individuals are mainly first time offenders. With regard to discontinuation, urine testing would seem to suggest a reduction in consumption but then again is this a matter of frequency or a real reduction in numbers.

Accordingly, the national survey in Portugal carried out in 1989 encountered similar problems to those reported above. Lifetime prevalence for the use of illegal drugs before imprisonment was respectively 62% in males and 55% in females. These figures drop to 48.5% and 20.5% respectively whilst in prison. The same caveat applies to those studies reported above.

It would appear that within the confines found within the prisons in the Russian Federation drug use continues unabated. It is also suggested that since this group form the majority group it is likely that initiation to drug use does indeed occur in prison; 17.9% was reported for the 1970s whereas the figure had increased to 57.6% for the 1980s.

Again, as in Portugal, the Spanish situation specifically refers to the number of inmates using drugs before entry into prison. In 1986, it was estimated that 70% of inmates were regular users of illegal drugs before entry while in 1998 this figure falls to around 50% but this now refers to those having problems related to the consumption of psychoactive substances. There is no information as yet on those starting use in prison but some data available on those stopping from the treatment demand indicator which is in place (see below).

Finally, the situation in the United Kingdom. Where drug use before entry had been ascertained it was noted that while in prison 27% of the cohort actually stopped using drugs while in prison. The reason given for such a reduction was incarceration itself and a number of other factors including the fear of detection via mandatory urine testing. However, information regarding first use in prison by previous non-drug users is scant. One study cited reported that 27% first tried heroin while in prison but akin to the Irish situation these might be drug users who have decided to try a new drug for varying reasons and not non-drug users starting up.

To summarise, it would appear that in most cases insufficient data is available on the drug habits of people before entering prison to allow for an assessment of whether drug use declines or increases on confinement. The limited data would tend to suggest a decline in consumption on incarceration but whether this is related to a reduction in frequency or real numbers still needs to be determined.

---

4. Patterns of use in prison

In the majority of countries participating in the study, that is Estonia, France, Ireland, the Netherlands, Malta, Portugal and the United Kingdom, a reduction in drug use in prison was reported. The reasons for this finding was mainly due to availability which in the case of France produced another problem in the form of the drug user taking anything that is made available which includes both illegal drugs and medicines. In the United Kingdom (England and Wales) a switch from hard to soft drugs (opiates to cannabis) is apparent, to compensate for decreased opiate availability. While the majority of prisoners in Ireland are reported to reduce their frequency of use while in prison, there is evidence that a small number of prisoners may be initiated into heroin use while in prison. Lack of access to drugs appears to be the main reason for a lower frequency of use. This phenomena, however, is also reported in the United Kingdom following the introduction of mandatory urine testing. The fact that cannabis is present for a longer time in body fluids, probably due to the deposition within fatty tissue, may result in detection long after use. Thus, the switch to heroin is a consequence of such tests and in turn lessens the chance of detection. It was a also noted that in prison the drug in question, heroin, is of such a poor quality that if detected on screening would fail more stringent tests of analysis, namely GCMS.

In the Netherlands, the data available to date has been accrued from those attending a methadone programme. The findings with regards to changes in patterns of drug use would appear similar to those reported for the United Kingdom and Ireland (see above) whilst the reasons given for such are rather different. It is argued that the methadone used on these treatment programmes is less effective as a result of lower dosing and type administered and thus inmates revert to other drugs such as cannabis and cocaine to potentiate the effects of the treatment.

To a limited extent, the data available from Spain, through the treatment demand indicator, would tend to suggest from those coming forward for treatment that drug use would appear to decrease in prison. However, there is no information as to whether these individuals also use in prison as cited above in the case of the Netherlands.

The findings from Estonia also support the notion of reduced drug use in prison, but the data only refer to one prison and are based solely on urine tests.

To summarise, frequency of drug use would seem to wane on imprisonment mainly due to a lack of availability. This in itself would appear to be a positive aspect of incarceration. However, there are resultant negative consequences. In the main, inmates now select strategies to offset this reduction in supply and will indulge in using anything that comes to hand, including medicines. Some now switch from heroin to cannabis while a number switch in the opposite direction, cannabis to heroin, in attempting to allay detection via urine testing. A small number first use heroin within the confines of prison.

5.   Routes of administration (risk behaviour)

As noted in the section above, frequency of drug use in prison decreased as a consequence of availability. To some extent, route of administration is also dependent on the availability of a particular drug. In addition, syringes and needles are not readily available and thus this added complication may result in other routes of administration even if a drug like heroin is within reach. In France, data from the ORS PACA European Survey noted that 35% of intravenous drug users (IDU) injected themselves while in prison while 6% had done so for the very first time. The figure for France is in the same range as that for England and Wales in that most of the published research indicated that between 25-33% of IDU population inject at some time while serving their prison sentence. Again, in three studies within the United Kingdom, it was reported that 25% and 6% of IDUs interviewed first injected while in prison while 7% of heroin users reported first injecting whilst in prison. However, in Ireland it would appear that initiation into injection use is significantly higher than that reported for France, England or Wales.

In Estonia, Greece and the Netherlands it would appear that injecting behaviour of the inmates is rather limited. This positive aspect is explained by the Netherlands from the findings that injecting behaviour before entry into prison is already very low, around 13%, and this is further supported by the low prevalence for HIV given at 4% of the drug using population. Moreover, the prevalence rates for HIV amongst IDUs in Greece range between 1.1% to 2.7% which would probably support the Dutch stance that users prefer to smoke, inhale or sniff their drugs of choice. On the other hand it may indeed reflect the type of user, possibly an informed user who is less likely to share injecting equipment knowing full well the consequences of such risk related behaviour. There again in Spain it has also been noted that a significant number of the drug users in prison coming forward for treatment prefer to inhale than inject but their HIV prevalence rates are high, around 32%. It is also acknowledged that these rates are higher than those found in the drug users coming forward for treatment in the general population (13%) but it is also suggested that these findings be viewed with some caution. In order to reduce the impact of sharing equipment, Greece supplies all inmates with bleach as part of their hygiene pack as recommended by the WHO guidelines on AIDS in prison and in Spain, syringe-exchange programmes are currently in operation in three prisons and a further three will come into being in three other centres.

In Estonia and Malta, there is no evidence to date to suggest the occurrence of intravenous drug use. It should be noted however, that in these two countries the data refer to a single prison of limited capacity. In the latter country, the prevalence of hepatitis C was estimated at 33% of the prison population, but no information was at hand to determine whether this was contracted before entry or in prison per se.

To summarise, it would appear that in prison the preferred route of administration was via, smoking, inhalation or sniffing the available drug. However, intravenous drug use does occur in prison although to a lesser extent. Inclusion of bleach in hygiene packs and syringe-exchange programmes are available in a limited number of institutions. The impact of these have to date been deemed positive.

6. Ongoing treatment

In the main drastic changes in ongoing treatment occur in most countries following incarceration. Two studies in France, the ORS PACA European Survey and the Ministry of Health Survey demonstrate that in the majority of users on some form of treatment, example, 73% of IDU's on methadone and 2% on substitute treatments, the trend is one of discontinuation of treatment on entry into prison. In the United Kingdom, due to the limited specialists units in operation the same outcome was the order of the day that is to say, treatment discontinuation on entry as the norm rather than the opposite was observed. In the case of Ireland this would also seem to be the case but the point is eloquently made that the programmes available in prison remain rather limited especially in the domain of female inmates.

In France, however, substitute treatment is available in prison but it is made abundantly clear that to obtain such treatment depends greatly on the medical views of the personnel within the particular establishment. To a similar extent, substitution treatment, in this case methadone, is available in all Spanish prisons. This is in line with policy which seeks to ensure the availability of such treatment standards as those found in the community, thus improving the probability of continuation of treatment on entry into prison. In line with such an approach, two other programmes have been implemented through which inmates may seek treatment. The first is an intrapenitentiary therapeutic cohort and the second, diversion of drug dependent inmates to community resources. These in turn have resulted in a significant number of inmates opting for treatment. In 1997, 6 606 received methadone treatment whereas in 1998 the figure stood at 10 577. The numbers were also on the increase for those diverted to community resources. In 1997, 1 974 used these resources while in 1998 the figure was 2 647. However, it would be of interest to know how many of these refer to single new treatment starts and how many refer to repeat starts by relapsers.

Abstinence is the mainstay in Greece, the Netherlands and Malta. Therefore, discontinuation of treatment would be the most likely outcome if the individual was on some sort of substitution programme before entry into prison. However, in the Netherlands, methadone is made available but the doses administered would appear to be lower than those used in the community. In the scientific literature it has been suggested that a dose in the order of 70mg is needed to sustain users on a programme and prevent them from seeking drugs elsewhere to top up the dose.

In Malta a lengthy process of assessment is required for continuation of care which makes opting for such treatment unlikely.

No form of substitution treatment is on offer within the Greek prison service, alternatively symptomatic relief is the order of the day.

There also limited treatment services on offer in the prison systems of Estonia and the Slovak Republic.

Portugal was the only other country besides Spain to report that the treatments available in the community were also available in prison. However, no indication was made as to whether inmates opted for treatment following imprisonment. This is rather crucial as it has already been demonstrated in the case of France, that those opting to continue or even start treatment are marginal even though treatment services exist.

To summarise, the majority of individuals undergoing some form of substitute treatment before entry into prison are more likely than not to discontinue treatment on incarceration.

---

7.   Discontinuation of drug use in prison

From what has followed in the earlier sections it would in the first instance appear that prison does have a positive effect on drug use in terms of stopping use. However, the subsequent ones would support the notion that this result has no bearing on the individuals motivation to stop drug use per se. The results of the ORS PACA European Survey in France suggested that persons have little knowledge of the services available or for that matter, any formal health education, making it highly unlikely that they opt for such services. It also acknowledged by the REESCOM Survey that successive prison terms make any prospect of life style change negligible.

Moreover, in England and Wales, the rationale for a reduction in drug use is in no manner related to the individual's motivation to change lifestyle but is rather the result of inaccessibility due to lack of availability of the drug per se or the resources to obtain it. In addition, the fear of detection also plays a significant role. However, in those that purport to stop drug use, the period is short lived because they view a prison stay as an opportunity to take a break from drug use rather than to stop use altogether.

In Ireland, it has been ascertained that even if inmates were motivated to cease their drug use the lack of services on offer would be prohibitive. The same would apply to Greece.

Those inmates serving a sentence of between 6 and 24 months in Malta and who fulfil strict inclusion criteria are the only ones able to attend the programme, and some 60% of this limited cohort suffer from major psychiatric disorders, which further complicates matters. In addition, all have to attend a three-month preparative stage before entry with the result that the drop out rate has now been severely curtailed.

Likewise, in the Netherlands it has been acknowledged that to motivate the drug user to seek treatment is a time consuming affair that often takes longer than one month. Thus, the strategy adopted is to increase the number of individuals following early intervention programmes. However, this too appears to occur late in the process as it was noted that all the places within such programmes are rarely fully occupied.

Penultimately, Estonia reported that 10% of inmates sought treatment while in treatment while in Greece and Portugal from the information accrued it was difficult to determine whether inmates are motivated or not stop their drug use.

Finally, in Spain it was reported that 24 201 inmates in 1998 received some form of treatment and that the number of treatment programmes started had increased. In addition, there were more heroin treatment programmes in prison than in the community which would imply that prison had a significant impact on the treatment of heroin users.

To summarise, prison on the whole does not motivate the individual to stop drug use. However, the one exception would appear to be Spain where the number of treatment starts had increased. In the other countries reporting a reduced drug use within prison, this would appear to be unrelated to the motivation of the drug user to stop per se but rather is a consequence of reduced availability, lack of resources to procure drugs or the fear of detection.

---

8. Executive Summary

In prisons in Estonia, France, Malta, the Netherlands, the Slovak Republic, England and Wales (United Kingdom) there is no evidence that inmates give up drug use.

The main finding with respect to changes in patterns of use are that in most participating countries prison reduced the frequency of use owing mainly to lack of availability and resources to obtain drugs and fear of detection. In turn, this may result in the use of anything available from illicit drugs to medicines with regard to the first two determinants.

In relation to routes of administration, intravenous drug users were less likely to inject while in prison than when free. The preferred routes included smoking, inhalation and sniffing. For those that did inject the lack of resources such as hygiene packs (except in Greece) and syringe-exchange programmes (except in Spain) may facilitate use in a risky manner with the resulting consequences.

Most prisons in the project member countries with the exception of Spain, Portugal and possibly France, do not provide an equivalence of service for the drug user to that found in the community. The result of which is a discontinuation of care under most circumstances. However, the fact that some countries provide most services that compliment those in the community does not itself guarantee the continuation or commencement of treatment.

In the vast majority of countries, prison has no positive effect on the motivation of the incarcerated drug user to stop drug use with the possible exception of Spain.

Finally, the availability of prison data in relation to drug use is limited and that on offer varies considerably between countries making comparability rather difficult at the best of times.

9. Recommendations

The single and most important service provision to the prison system as it stands would be one in which the drug user is motivated to stop drug use. In addition, it would also be advisable to provide complimentary services such as harm reduction, continuation of treatment and the prevention of starting drug use.

It would also be of use if an early intervention approach such as that practiced in the Netherlands is given serious thought, especially in those countries that lack service provision within the confines of prison. In those that do provide extensive coverage, it might be of interest to review the policy and strategy adopted by Spain.

A limited study should be carried out to determine the negative attributes of prison on the motivation of the imprisoned drug user to stop drug use. This in turn may provide the framework for the basis of the type of service suggested above.

A final important consideration would be the design of a common methodology through which it would be possible to collect reliable information on a regular basis on drug use in prison in the countries concerned.

10. References

This reference list pertains solely to the core documents used in the compilation of this report. Any studies cited in the text concerning the participating countries may be found in the respective country reports.

Drug use in Prison Project. P-PG/Epid (98) 16 rev.

Report of the Paris meeting (March 1999). P-PG/Epid (99) 9E.

Report of the Strasbourg meeting (June 1999). P-PG/Epid (99) 12 E.

Guidelines. P-PG/Epid (99) 14 E.

Council of Europe, Committee Of Ministers, Recommendation No. R (98) 7 of the Committee of Ministers to member states concerning the ethical and organisational aspects of health care in prison.

European Monitoring Centre for Drugs and Drug Addiction (EMCDDA) extended Annual Report 1999.

COUNTRY REPORTS

Estonian Report
Drug Use by Prisoners

Sirje Sepalaan

There was an extensive survey among inmates in May and June 1999 in four Estonian prisons. We distributed 1 150 questionnaires and 706 of them were returned. Extra questions were included in the questionnaire, which are in this report. The summary will not be ready until the end of the year.

A similar survey was carried out last summer among fifty-four adolescents in Viljandi prison. All urine tests were negative. Seventeen persons (31.5%) had used different drugs before prison. None of them use drugs in prison. Two boys (3.7%) only mentioned alcohol use. Thirty-three (61.1%) were smokers and nine (16.7%) received different medicines on prescription.

In August 1999, there were fifty-five adolescents in Viljandi prison. Seven (12.7%) of them were drug users before prison and eight (14,5%) were drug addicts. None of the inmates started using drugs in prison, but if drugs were accessible then four boys (7.3%) would use them.

Drug use in prison took place by exchange (benzodiazepines or solvents). No syringes or needles were found this year. The administration does not supply injecting material. Before imprisonment, three boys were treated in psychiatric institutions. In prison the doctor prescribed sedatives and analgesics. Five boys are motivated to stop using drugs and two are not.

The first drug-free department in Estonian prisons will open this Autumn in Viljandi. Personnel have been hired and trained. A kitchen and rooms are partially equipped. At present five inmates want to go there.

French report

Charlotte Trabut

Contributions

This summary report has been prepared by Charlotte Trabut, special consultant to the Interministerial Task-Force to Combat Drugs and Drug Abuse (*Mission interministérielle de lutte contre la drogue et la toxicomanie*), on the basis of:

1. the work by Dr Rotily of the Provence-Alpes-Côte d'Azur Regional Health Observatory (ORS PACA), who has focused on transmission of infectious diseases in prison and, more generally, on drug use, risk behaviour and reduction of risks in prison. Dr Rotily has undertaken a number of studies within the European network for the prevention of HIV/AIDS and viral hepatitis in prisons (European Community). His most recent survey, carried out in four prisons, has not yet been published;

2. the work of Sylvie Stankoff, who is in charge of drug dependency issues within the French prisons service (*Direction de l'Administration Pénitentiare*);

3. that done by Hélène Morfini, Colette Parpillon and Isabelle Tortay of the Ministry of Health;

4. the work of Patricia Bouhnik, Elisabeth Jacob, Isabelle Maillard and Sylviane Touz of the RESSCOM research laboratory on the subject of drug users released from prison, based on interviews with users attending counselling centres (1999), commissioned by the Ministry of Justice and the Ministry of Health. This study has not yet been published.

For further information, the following texts could be consulted:

–   the European recommendations issued by the European Network for the prevention of HIV/AIDS and viral hepatitis in prisons (1999);

–   an article and European statistics on use of drugs in prison by Michel Rotily and Claire Delorme (1999);

–   an article by Michel Rotily and Caren Weiland on risk behaviour and HIV transmission in Europe's prisons (1999);

–   a study of treatment with drug substitutes in prisons conducted by the Ministry of Health in 1998;

– a study of inmates' state of health on committal to prison carried out by the statistical department of the Ministry of Health in 1998.

The figures cited in this summary report have been obtained from the above sources and from two as yet unpublished surveys carried out in 1999 at the request of the Ministry of Health and the Ministry of Justice:

• A European survey of four French prisons and of prisons in seven other countries, using the same protocol, carried out by the ORS PACA. 1 212 prisoners, representing between 62% and 87% of the total number of inmates depending on the prison, answered a questionnaire on a voluntary, anonymous basis.

• The 1999 RESSCOM survey of drug users released from prison, based on interviews of users attending counselling centres, commissioned by the Ministry of Justice and the Ministry of Health. The respondents were intravenous drug users - first offenders or recidivists - released from prison less than a year previously. Eighty-five people were interviewed, 35 of them on more than one occasion. The majority had been released from a short-stay prison (*maison d'arrêt*) and had not decided to give up drugs. They came from twenty different prisons, a sufficiently broad selection to be representative. These users - aged from 24 to 40 - live in extremely precarious circumstances. Although it should be borne in mind that the uniformity of the interviewees' profiles may be an indication that the interviewers had a somewhat biased view of public health policy and the realities of prison life, the number of interviews, the fact that some respondents were "followed up" for more than four months and, above all, the precision and degree of concordance of the data lead to the conclusion that this survey constitutes a sound source of information.

Neither of these two surveys, on which this summary report draws to a large extent, has yet been published.

1. Brief description of the prison system and of the organisation of health care in prisons

Background and objectives

Criminal law

In principle, the law prohibits use of drugs but allows for the possibility of treatment with drug substitutes in the case of users wishing to cure themselves of their addiction. Drug users are guaranteed anonymous treatment free of charge.

The concept of "use"; comparison with other European countries

"Use" means "consumption" of drugs. In France, in contrast to many other European countries, the concept of possession for personal use does not exist. However, in practice those arrested while in possession of small quantities of drugs are frequently treated as "users" if there are no signs that they are dealing.

The question whether use of drugs should be a punishable offence continues to be a subject of public debate. Detractors of existing French law criticise it for confusing the issue by treating drug users at times as people who are ill and at times as offenders.

However, in this sphere little can be learned from comparisons between countries if mere knowledge of the law is not supplemented with a study of police and judicial practice.

Treatment orders

When a drug user, even a minor, is brought before the public prosecutor, the prosecutor may decide to stay prosecution and order the person concerned to follow a course of treatment.

Where the prosecutor decides to bring charges, the user is liable to a one-year prison sentence and a fine of 25 000 francs, or only one of these two penalties (Article L 628 of the Public Health Code).

But the trial court may also decide to:

- give a suspended sentence, with or without putting the accused on probation, and make it compulsory for the person concerned to obtain treatment;
- issue a community service order, combined with an order to undergo treatment;
- discharge a convicted person without imposing a penalty if that person can prove that he or she has sought treatment pending the judgment[1].

---

[1]   A bill currently before parliament envisages offering public prosecutors another solution, that of "*composition pénale*", where for certain less serious offences, to which drug use has been added under a parliamentary amendment, the prosecutor may stay prosecution in exchange for the offender's agreement to make reparation, which may, for example, take the form of payment of a sum of money or performance of unpaid community service. This reform has not yet been passed.

An analysis of practice with regard to drug users shows that, although the number of arrests has risen fast since 1990 (80% of arrests are for use of cannabis), the number of users prosecuted is tending to decline.

A user sentenced to prison may be allowed to benefit from various measures (semi-detention, outside placement, conditional release) combined with compulsory treatment.

Drug use in prison

Prison statistics

187 prisons

- As at 1 January 1999, there were 53 000 prisoners, including 20 000 being detained pending trial.

- The average length of imprisonment is tending to increase (8.3 months in 1999 compared with 7 months in 1990) because of an increase in longer sentences.

- 75 000 prisoners were released in 1998, including 25 000 regular drug users.

Epidemiological data

For a number of years, the prison service has been confronted with the problem of the high number of drug users in prison. Because of changes in judicial practice, these are primarily ordinary criminals with a drug problem, not people serving a sentence for drug use. In 1986 a national survey showed that 10.6% of persons committed to prison admitted to having taken drugs at least twice a month over the three months preceding the date of imprisonment. In 1997 a survey of inmates' state of health at the time of committal showed that over 30% of those committed had made regular use of drugs or of psychoactive medication, diverted from its proper use, during the year preceding the date of imprisonment. This survey confirmed that drug-dependent behaviour is very frequent in the prison population.

Among the survey's findings it can be noted that:

- 32% of those committed to prison stated that they had made prolonged, regular use of at least one drug (illegal drugs or medicines) during the year preceding their incarceration. Half of these were opiates consumers;

- 6.2% stated that they had used drugs by intravenous injection during the year preceding their committal;

Table 1: Judicial practice in respect of mere users (excluding addict pushers, traffickers and persons charged with other drug-related offences)

Year	Number of arrests	Treatment orders	Number of convictions	of which: unsuspended sentence	of which: discharged without penalty	of which: community service orders	of which: educational measures (minors)
1990	24 856	3 541	4 647	1 113 (24%)[1] 3.5 months[2]	107	98	177
1991	34 311	Not available	4 086	1 031 (25%) 3.5 months	94	131	204
1992	41 549	4 935	3 887	1 023 (26%) 3.5 months	111	112	172
1993	38 189	6 149	4 043	1103 (27%) 3.1 months	126	81	139
1994	44 261	7 678	2 663	600 (23%) 3.2 months	111	160	48
1995	52 112	8 630	1 375	298 (22%) 3.6 months	27	70	41
1996	56 144	8 812	2 979	603 (20%) 2.7 months	77	183	127
1997	70 444	8 052	3 368	494 (15%) 2.4 months	134	245	203

[1] Unsuspended prison sentences as a % of all convictions.

[2] Average length of unsuspended sentences.

31

- 33% admitted to excess alcohol consumption;

- 78% smoked (18% more than twenty cigarettes a day);

- 17% stated that they were being treated with psychotropic substances.

Given this state of affairs, the prisons service's aim is to influence both supply, by taking measures to prevent drugs from entering and circulating within prisons, and demand, through improved care for drug users.

Organisation of health care

The care structure in prison

Since 1994, the Ministry of Health has taken charge of prisoner health care through the public hospitals service. Within this structure, treatment of drug-dependent behaviour is the responsibility of the psychiatric team assigned to a given prison, which works in close co-operation with a team responsible for physical care and with the prison service's social and educational workers.

In a minority of prisons – those most recently built – prisoner health care is sub-contracted to the private sector. An audit is currently being carried out to determine whether the private sector should continue to provide these services or be replaced by the public sector.

Treatment of drug dependency

1.   In sixteen large short-stay prisons, specialist treatment centres for drug addicts have been set up inside the prison under the medical authority of the senior medical officer in charge of the psychiatric service. These centres are responsible for identifying drug-dependent prisoners, monitoring their progress and preparing them for release, but also for co-ordinating all of the measures taken in this field. They therefore provide more all-round help than the medical service.

In the 170 other prisons, external specialist treatment centres for drug addicts are called upon to take action inside the prisons to supplement the care provided by the prison medical service and to prepare drug-dependent prisoners for release.

2.   In seven prisons, pre-release units, which house drug-dependent prisoners nearing the date of their release, have also been established. These units offer prisoners with drug problems, who have volunteered to be transferred there, a four-week course of group treatment (at most ten persons) with the aim of preparing them for release.

Cracking down on smuggling of drugs into prison

Since 1997, the police have been encouraged to perform checks for drugs in prison visiting facilities under the authority of the public prosecution service. Many such checks were organised in 1997 and 1998. As a general rule, the quantities of drugs found are small, but the checks appear to have a genuinely dissuasive effect within the prisons. They will continue and will be supplemented with preventive measures targeting prisoners' families in 1999 and the year 2000.

2. Basis of a reply to the question "What effect does prison have on drug use?"

2.1 Effect in terms of prisoners' stopping or starting drug use

Statistics on continuation of drug use while in prison

- In a 1992 survey of 432 prisoners, conducted by the ORS PACA in Marseille, 20% of the prisoners questioned stated that they had made intravenous use of drugs (primarily heroin) in the course of their lives, and 51% of these had shared needles.

- In another ORS PACA survey in Marseille, carried out in 1996 with 574 prisoners, 23% stated that they had already injected themselves in prison in the course of their lives. According to this survey, 13% of those who had been active injectors during the twelve months preceding their committal to prison (nine prisoners out of sixty-eight) stated that they had made intravenous use of drugs during their first three months in prison.

- A European survey was conducted in 1997/98 in four French prisons and in prisons in seven other countries, using the same protocol. The French part of this survey was carried out by Dr Rotily on behalf of the ORS PACA. 1 212 prisoners, representing between 62% and 87% of the total number of inmates, depending on the prison, volunteered to take part. Respondents were guaranteed anonymity. 32% of the respondents stated that they had consumed, but not injected, illegal drugs while in prison; 35% of the active intravenous drug users (IDUs) had injected themselves during their stay in prison.

Table 2: Drugs and poisonous substances inhaled, smoked or swallowed before and during imprisonment

Substance	Percentage of prisoners having used the substance during the 12 months preceding committal	Percentage of prisoners having used the substance while in prison
Cocaine	18% (56% IDUs)	7% (26% IDUs)
Crack	3% (13% IDUs)	2% (9% IDUs)
Cannabis	37% (73% IDUs)	26% (55% IDUs)
Ecstasy	9% (25% IDUs)	3% (14% IDUs)
Amphetamines	6% (21% IDUs)	3% (13% IDUs)
LSD, acid, hallucinogens	7% (21% IDUs)	3% (13% IDUs)
Subutex, Temgesic	8% (42% IDUs)	7% (35% IDUs)
Moscontin or Skenan	2% (13% IDUs)	1% (7% IDUs)
Methadone	2% (12% IDUs)	1% (4% IDUs)

- In 1999, RESSCOM was commissioned by the Ministry of Justice and the Ministry of Health to carry out a survey of drug users released from prison, by interviewing users attending counselling centres.

The interviews showed that drug use in prison is a long-standing phenomenon, dating back to the early eighties.

Its prevalence varies depending on the institution (the phenomenon is more significant in large institutions and in short-stay prisons).

The substances used have varied over time (amphetamines, barbiturates, cannabis, heroine, rohypnol, cocaine and, more recently, Subutex, crack and Skenan).

Cannabis was already in circulation in the prisons during the early eighties, as was heroin, but to a more limited extent and through better organised dealing networks. Respondents spoke of prisoners who had made regular use of heroin throughout a long prison term. Over half of the respondents said they had consumed heroin at least once while in prison.

A number of heroin users had discovered Subutex in prison. Respondents stated, however, that decisions to stop prescribing Subutex in certain institutions on account of problems with peddling had had no effect on consumption of the substance by inmates because it was smuggled into the prisons.

The authors conclude that prisons are not sealed off from the outside world. The same substances as are available outside are to be found inside, with the same regional variations in patterns of use. Their findings are pessimistic. They point out that it is far rarer today than in the past for someone to go through prison without consuming all sorts of psychoactive substances, and that certain users discover new substances (medicines, Subutex) while in prison. "Not only is it clear that prison is not a place where people solve their drug problems, but it can also be seen to be less and less a place where they break with their habit, even temporarily. Abstinence while in prison is more a matter of personal choice than an option worked on with the institution."

Summary

Drug use remains a fact of life in prison and reflects changes in patterns of consumption in the outside world. Prisons are not sealed off. Imprisonment does not have any noticeable effect on whether people stop taking drugs or continue to use them.

2.2 Effect on patterns of use: types of drugs, regularity, frequency, quantity consumed

• Results of the RESSCOM survey of drug users released from prison

Why and how do people use drugs in prison?

Drugs are a means of fighting boredom and enduring prison, of dealing with the hardships of prison life.

Some users describe a constant search for drugs: "If I could get some every day when I'm inside ... You get bored to death, pills, dope, you take anything that's going ... Getting stoned becomes a pastime." (Marc, aged 28)

The authors speak of prisoners' desire to be constantly high on something, without any particular preference as to what and without any distinction being drawn between legal and illegal substances. Prisoners take whatever is available. In this context imprisonment frequently leads to addiction to certain medicinal substances.

Lastly, inmates sometimes take drugs to help themselves overcome a crisis (bad news, conviction and sentencing, violence, the suicide of a fellow prisoner, etc). In such circumstances, they may relapse after a period of withdrawal.

People take greater risks inside prison than outside

Just as the health precautions taken by drug-using prisoners are very crude (see 2.3), they often show a lack of discernment as to the quantities and nature of the substances which they consume. It is not infrequent for prisoners to obtain illegal drugs in exchange for medicines, prescribed to a prisoner or secured by other means.

Moreover, one respondent described how a fellow prisoner had suffered from an overdose after taking a mix of medicinal substances.

In conclusion, the authors stress that the frontier between "drugs" and psychoactive medicines has completely disappeared. They are critical of the policy governing access to treatment. Without calling into doubt its ethical basis (encouraging a responsible attitude in patients, access to the same forms of treatment as are available outside prison), they think that it does not take sufficient account of user habits and lifestyles outside prison. They take the view that patients are not given enough individual support. "These shortcomings make treatment with drug substitutes a mere technique, rather than an attempt to help establish conditions conducive to a change in the user's lifestyle. ... Where the situation and the available resources do not permit individual care and follow-up, the ingredients are at hand for people to remain in prison, stuck in their old habits, without any hope of change, and even in a state of absolute despair."

Desired effects according to the substance used

Cannabis for relaxation; Subutex and heroin for a "high"; medicinal substances to dull one's mind.

Crack is a subject of controversy, since coming down from a trip is such a painful experience and the supply is so uncertain.

Some inmates maintain that drugs do not produce such satisfying effects in prison as they do outside, whereas others claim that their sensations are heightened in prison.

Dealing with the craving

When they suffered withdrawal symptoms respondents first sought to procure the same substance as they were taking outside prison.

"If you don't have your treatment, you can find it in the exercise yard if you want."

Some users, whose symptoms were not fully relieved by the substitute treatment prescribed to them, took other drugs to satisfy their craving.

The proximity of the peddlers, the influence of other users, maintenance of social ties through relationships largely based on barter

Users are in contact with dealers whom they knew outside or whom they met during a previous term in prison. "The peddlers spot you fast."

"I really wanted to come off drugs, but it was very hard ... When I knew there was stuff around I didn't hesitate, although I hadn't touched it for six months." (Youssef, 32)

All the respondents mention that dealing goes on quite openly, speak of the signs whereby dealers and users recognise one another and note an increase in drug dealing in recent years.

At a more general level, relationships in prison are founded on exchanges: "If you have something to exchange, you can get whatever you want." Illegal substances have a high barter value and can be swapped for other goods. Cannabis, heroin, Subutex and Skenan are worth three or four times as much as they are outside.

Given this situation, the availability of health care and the possibility of having a treatment prescribed are described as one means of procuring something of value to exchange.

The hierarchy that exists between groups who know one another outside is reconstituted inside. In particular, the different "jobs" associated with dealing re-appear inside prison.

Abstainers

Although they appear to be a minority, some inmates still see prison as an opportunity to "take a break, to recover physically". These are mostly heroin addicts.

Other users suffer forced abstinence for lack of money.

However, the authors point out that none of the respondents had abstained fully from drugs during their time in prison.

Summary

For lack of genuine individual support, in particular during a course of medical treatment, prison does not bring about a change of lifestyle; it therefore has little impact on drug usage patterns. It enables a minority of highly motivated inmates to take a break from their habit. It tends to lead to indiscriminate mass consumption of drugs and medicines, without any distinction being drawn between illegal drugs and psychoactive medicines.

2.3 Effect on routes of drug administration: inhalation, smoking, injection, needle sharing, observance of standards of hygiene

- The survey conducted in Marseille in 1996 showed that 13% of active IDUs had injected themselves while in prison and nearly half of these users (44%) had shared needles.

- Results of the ORS PACA European survey conducted in 1997-98 in four French prisons and seven prisons in other countries, using the same protocol

Injection (mainly of heroin)

Only the active IDUs (those who had used drugs intravenously during the twelve months preceding their committal to prison) stated that they had continued to inject themselves while in prison.

This gives the following percentages:

- of the entire population of respondents, 3.5% stated that they had injected themselves at some time while in prison, and 0.6% had begun to do so there.

- of all IDUs (who numbered 150 or 13% of respondents), 35% had injected themselves while in prison and 6% had done so for the first time there.

- of the active IDUs (who numbered 103 or 8.6% of respondents), 42% had injected themselves in prison in the course of their lives, 28% while serving their current sentence, 12% had done so more than twenty times, 7% had injected themselves for the first time while in prison, 10% had shared equipment in prison in the course of their lives, 9% had shared equipment when they last injected themselves in prison, and 15% had used bleach to disinfect their equipment.

The authors conclude that, in view of the high rates of HIV and hepatitis C seropositivity, especially among IDUs (15% and 43% respectively), prisoners' continuing failure to take precautions when injecting themselves, and the fact that sexual relations in prison are often unprotected, prison, which leads to only a small decrease in drug use, can be seen to be conducive to the transmission of infectious diseases.

- Results of the RESSCOM survey of drug users released from prison

Inhaling Subutex

Respondents stated that the prevailing route of administration of Subutex in prison was inhalation, since it was difficult to obtain syringes. They maintained that all prisoners taking Subutex, including those following a course of treatment, sniffed the substance. The heroin addicts, in particular, had all started inhaling Subutex in prison.

Skenan is also inhaled.

Injecting

Although injecting is described as a marginal activity among inmates, it is practised in prisons all over France mainly by heroin users (Subutex and Skenan may exceptionally be injected), and over one-third of the respondents had injected themselves at least once while in prison.

Observance of standards of hygiene

Used syringes are spirited away from the infirmary or even retrieved from dustbins. Other syringes are obtained from outside the prison by methods which the respondents did not reveal.

In prison, a syringe is often shared by a more or less limited group of users (prisoners housed in the same cell or a larger group).

Injection equipment may also be exchanged for injectable substances, with the result that syringes circulate widely. In that case inmates do not know who used a syringe before them. Where a syringe does not circulate among a number of users, it is always reused by its owner. Inmates who avoid sharing a syringe do so out of concern to safeguard a rare, valuable object, not for health reasons.

A new syringe may be used for several months. Syringes are cleaned with water or bleach.

Although respondents were aware of the risks, their accounts showed a changed perception of them in prison. Risk was seen as something one had to live with, the primary concern being to succeed in injecting oneself without being detected.

Two respondents thought they had contracted hepatitis C while in prison.

Yet, the drug users interviewed were not in favour of distributing syringes in prisons, describing such a measure as "illogical" and "incomprehensible" for prisoners who were at the same time being punished for taking drugs.

Summary

Although injecting is practised by a small minority of inmates, almost exclusively active IDUs, none of France's prisons is free of the phenomenon. Prisoners, whose primary concern is to lay their hands on the substance and the equipment, show little regard for standards of hygiene. Prison is conducive to risk-taking and to the transmission of infectious diseases.

2.4 Effect in terms of medical treatment: discontinuation or beginning of treatment

- Results of the ORS PACA European survey performed in 1997/98 in four French prisons and seven prisons in other countries, using the same protocol

Half of the active IDUs had consulted a specialist treatment centre during the twelve months preceding their committal to prison.

Exactly the same proportion had consulted a prison doctor about their drug problem. Of these, 10% had been prescribed methadone and 27% Subutex.

10% of the active IDUs were taking methadone just before their committal to prison, and 34% Subutex. In prison, 73% of the IDUs taking methadone, and 63% of those taking Subutex, had discontinued the treatment.

Lastly, in absolute terms, the percentage of drug users being treated with substitutes is more than halved in prison.

- Results of the Ministry of Health survey of treatment with drug substitutes in prison, carried out in 1998

A questionnaire was sent to the medical services (somatic and psychiatric) of all prisons in France.

The questions posed concerned the number of courses of treatment started or discontinued on committal to prison, the number of courses of treatment being followed at the time of the survey and the percentage of inmates receiving drug substitutes, methods of monitoring the health and welfare of inmates being treated, methods of preparing inmates for release and of ensuring continuation of treatment after release.

Results: 2% of inmates receive treatment with drug substitutes (1.7% Subutex and 0.3% methadone). This is clearly a small percentage of the population potentially concerned by this type of treatment, and the underlying situations differ considerably from one institution to another, depending on whether or not the local medical team is in favour of using substitutes.

It should be noted that in France it is possible to start a course of treatment with drug substitutes in prison.

However, this remains a marginal phenomenon.

The percentage of inmates already following a course of treatment with drug substitutes at the time of their committal to prison is also low: 4.1%, to be compared with the 14.4% of new inmates who are active opiate users and the 6.2% who are active IDUs.

The Ministry of Health gives the following explanations for this low figure:

- at the time of their committal few new inmates declare that they are following a course of treatment;

- treatment with drug substitutes facilitates users' social rehabilitation, and therefore fewer of those who have received treatment are to be found in prison. The drug users found in prison are hence those who are least well integrated into society and they do not have access to health care outside prison. If credit is given to this explanation, imprisonment should, according to the Ministry of Health's reasoning, be an opportunity to raise the number of users undergoing treatment to a level nearer that observed outside prison (according to estimates, 60 000 of the 160 000 opiates users outside prison are being treated with drug substitutes).

However, imprisonment is more likely to result in discontinuation of treatment. 22% of new inmates taking Subutex and 13% of those taking methadone had ceased treatment within eight weeks of their incarceration.

Conversely, continuation of treatment on release is fairly well guaranteed: 95% of former prisoners taking methadone and 79% of those taking Subutex receive medical support on leaving prison.

- Results of the RESSCOM survey of drug users released from prison

Respondents' accounts corroborated the findings of the survey on treatment with drug substitutes in prison

Overall, treatment tends to be reserved for those already taking drug substitutes at the time of their committal to prison. This is the main reason why people change treatment in prison. Respondents also complained that doctors' and prisons' attitudes varied greatly.

"In prison some people are regarded as patients and others as drug abusers." The survey showed that drug users find the situation incomprehensible. Whether Subutex is obtained lawfully or purchased in the street, it is just as frequently misused (injected or inhaled; combined with other drugs, in particular cocaine; taken in excessive doses). But some people have access to this medicine and others do not, a state of affairs which is perceived as an inconsistency of the medical system.

The survey also showed that owing to widespread use of psychoactive medication, prescribed by prison doctors, some prisoners – in particular women – become dependent after a stay in prison. Respondents also reported an increase in traffic in such medication in recent years.

Summary

Although prison allows the most socially deprived drug users to have access to health care, it results in discontinuation of treatment with drug substitutes on the basis of a distinction (which prisoners regard as artificial) between patients already taking drug substitutes at the time of their committal and other users who cannot show a medical prescription. Prison leads to mass consumption of psychoactive medication.

2.5 Effect on user motivation to give up drugs or seek treatment

- Results of the ORS PACA European survey performed in 1997/98 in four French prisons and seven prisons in other countries, using the same protocol

The report stresses that only a small percentage of respondents (28%) were vaccinated against hepatitis B, although 79% of them said they would be willing to be vaccinated if offered the option.

Vaccination is in fact available in prison, but not many inmates know this. Similarly, the survey showed that few prisoners know that condoms are available from the medical service.

At a more general level, the authors conclude that prisoners' scant health education and the lack of information about the various treatment and prevention possibilities available in prison reduce the potential impact of a stay in prison in terms of access to health care.

- Results of the RESSCOM survey of drug users released from prison

It should be noted that some of the respondents belong to the category of users most at risk from all points of view and many of them have been in prison many times.

In these circumstances, prison can be viewed as a means of "saving lives" by slowing down the process of general deterioration affecting certain drug users. And yet it does not seem capable of bringing about a change of lifestyle.

"You go into prison and when you come out you're still the same, nothing has changed." (Olivier, aged 35)

Successive prison terms tend to make any prospect of a change of lifestyle and any chance of rehabilitation more illusory.

In the case of other inmates, prison is a sudden disruption of their lives with marked adverse effects on their social integration and drug-related behaviour: loss of outside support, of employment, of accommodation and contact with new substances circulating inside prison.

Nevertheless, most of the respondents said that prison was the only place where they had access to education, training and work; it is also their only opportunity to have access to health care.

However, the authors' overall conclusion is a pessimistic one: prison's effect on the will to rid oneself of addiction is more negative than positive. "Prison strengthens, slows, gives new impetus to or preserves their way of life ... It

43

does not fundamentally change the situation. In particular, we consider that prison tends to be even less a place of rehabilitation or transition for women than it is for men; it is a place which finally wears away the few resources which inmates may have left."

Summary

Prison has scarcely any effect on prisoners' motivation to change their behaviour in general and their drug-use habits in particular. It tends to rigidify, or even strengthen, individual behaviour patterns, and it worsens isolation and integration difficulties.

Nevertheless, for many socially deprived drug users it remains the only opportunity of gaining access to health care, and it should therefore be regarded as a strategic place for providing information on risk reduction and health education.

Greek Report

Greek Organisation Against Drugs (OKANA)

1. Epidemiology and background information

In Greece, there are twenty-eight prisons with a total housing capacity of 4 502 prisoners. The number of prisoners on 1 January 1999 was 7 280. Two of these prisons are therapeutic (prison hospital and mental clinic), three are agricultural (open) prisons, three are juvenile prisons and one is a woman's prison. It should be noted that the four largest prisons have a total housing capacity of 1 716 prisoners and the number of prisoners on 1 January 1999 was 3 476.

The prison population on 1 January in recent years has been as follows : 2 815 in 1979; 3 559 in 1984; 4 582 in 1989; 5 275 in 1992; 6 555 in 1993; 6 884 in 1994; 5 695 in 1995; 5 897 in 1996; 5 313 in 1997 and 6 150 in 1998. The sudden increase in the number of prisoners in 1993 was due to the influx of Albanian refugees while the decrease after 1994 is attributed to a series of beneficial provisions targeted to encounter the problem of overcrowding in prisons. Table 1 shows in detail the prison population on 1 January over the last six years. In this time period, the percentage of drug offenders among the imprisoned population ranges from 33.2% to 37.6%.

Information on demographic characteristics, legal status, and drug use in the prison population is available from a study carried out in 1995 at Korydallos prison (Athens) which had a population of 1 183 (Table 2). 31% of the prisoners were injecting drug users (IDUs) and 20.7% of the sample (68.4% of IDUs) admitted having shared needles.

Table 1: Prison population in Greece

	1994	1995	1996	1997	1998	1999
Total capacity	4 302	4 302	4 302	4 332	4,332	4 502
Prison population	6 884	5 695	5 897	5 313	6,150	7 280
Prisoners awaiting trial	2 027 (29.4%)	1 700 (29.9%)	1 992 (33.8%)	1 726 (32.5%)	1,953 (31.7%)	2 554 (35.1%)
Foreign prisoners	Unknown	Unknown	1 702 (28.9%)	2 011 (37.9%)	2,477 (40.2%)	3 372 (46.3%)
Female prisoners	321 (4.7%)	240 (4.2%)	204 (3.5%)	195 (3.7%)	244 (3.9%)	285 (3.9%)
Juvenile prisoners	382 (5.5%)	310 (5.4%)	327 (5.5%)	360 (6.8%)	440 (7.1%)	595 (8.2%)
Prisoners with drug related offences	2 501 (36.3%)	1 890 (33.2%)	2 171 (36.8%)	1 998 (37.6%)	2,280 (37.0%)	2 648 (36.3%)
Prisoners with death sentences [1]	11 (0.16%)	10 (0.18%)	9 (0.15%)	7 (0.13%)	6 (0.09%)	6 (0.08%)
Prisoners with life imprisonment	386 (5.6%)	379 (6.7%)	411 (7.0%)	404 (7.6%)	397 (6.4%)	393 (5.4%)

(1) Death sentences are not executed

Table 2: Demographic history, legal status and drug use behaviour of 1183 prisoners from Korydallos prison, Athens (1995).

Variable	N	(%)
Gender		
Male	1 008	(85.3)
Female	74	(14.7)
Race		
White	1 136	(96.3)
Black	37	(3.1)
Other	7	(0.6)
Age		
<21	74	(6.3)
21-25	143	(12.1)
25-30	241	(20.5)
31-40	407	(34.6)
>40	313	(26.5)
Legal status		
Awaiting trial	533	(45.6)
Imprisoned	598	(51.1)
Both	39	(3.3)
Intravenous drug use		
Yes	363	(30.8)
No	815	(69.2)
Needle-sharing		
Yes	242	(20.7)
No	112	(9.6)
N.A	815	(69.7)

(Source: Quarterly Edition of the Hellenic Centre for the Control of AIDS and STDs)

A cumulative total of 1 882 AIDS cases was reported in Greece on 31 December 1998. 1 852 sufferers were adult/adolescents. In 1998, the incidence rate was 8.75 per million of the population. AIDS cases by year of diagnosis reported in Greece on 31 December 1998 are presented in Table 3. Among the infectious categories, IDUs and homo/bi-sexual IDUs account for 3.3% and 0.6% of the total respectively (Table 4).

Table 3: AIDS cases by year of diagnosis reported in Greece on 31 December 1998

Year of diagnosis	Aids cases		Incidence rate (per million population)
	N	(%)	
1982	2	(0.1)	0.20
1983	5	(0.3)	0.51
1984	5	(0.3)	0.51
1985	16	(0.9)	1.61
1986	23	(1.2)	2.31
1987	61	(3.2)	6.10
1988	73	(3.9)	7.27
1989	106	(5.6)	10.50
1990	142	(7.5)	13.97
1991	183	(9.7)	17.86
1992	191	(10.2)	18.50
1993	169	(9.0)	16.28
1994	213	(11.3)	20.43
1995	211	(11.2)	20.18
1996	230	(12.2)	21.95
1997	159	(8.5)	15.14
1998	93	(4.9)	8.75
Total	1882	(100.0)	

(Source: Quarterly Edition of the Hellenic Centre for the Control of AIDS and STDs in Greece)

On 1 January 1999, there were ten HIV positive cases of whom none were women in Greek prisons. Studies of bloodborne viruses prevalent among Greek prisoners have been targeted either at high risk groups (IDUs or drug users in general) (2,3,4) or at the total prison population and have identified low rates of HIV-1 infection (Table 5). A survey carried out in 1995, in Korydallos prison (Athens) with voluntary testing and risk factor elicitation on 1 183 prisoners, identified a prevalence of 1.1% for HIV-1 (8 out of 13 HIV positive cases were already known), 27.5% for HCV and 48.7% for HBV. Between 1986 and 1989, HIV-1 among imprisoned IDUs ranged from 1.1% to 2.7% (2) and subsequent studies identified a prevalence of 0.54% (3) in 1991-92 and of 0.27% in 1994-95 (4). High prevalence rates for HCV and HBV among IDUs have been reported by studies carried out in two prisons in Athens and Patras (3,4) and indicated an epidemic of hepatitis B and C among imprisoned IDUs.

Table 4: Adult and Adolescent AIDS cases (>12 years of age) by transmission group and sex reported by 31 December 1998

Transmission Group	Males		Females		Total	
	N	(%)	N	(%)	N	(%)
Homo-/bisexual males	1 093	(67.5)	-	-	1 093	(59.0)
IDUs	54	(3.3)	18	(7.8)	72	(3.9)
Homo-/bisexual IDUs	9	(0.6)	-	-	9	(0.5)
Haemophiliacs/ Coagulation disorder	99	(6.1)	5	(2.2)	104	(5.6)
Transfusion recipients	31	(1.9)	25	(10.8)	56	(3.0)
Heterosexual contact	144	(8.9)	159	(68.5)	303	(16.4)
Other/Undetermined	190	(11.7)	25	(10.8)	215	(11.6)
Total	1 468	(100.0)	206	(100.0)	1 674	(100.0)

(Source: Quarterly Edition of the Hellenic Centre for the Control of AIDS and STDs in Greece)

49

Table 5: A study on the prevalence of blood borne viruses in Greek prisons

Place/ year of study	Korydallos (Athens) and Ag.Stefanos (Patras) prisons/ 1991-92 (3)	Korydallos prison (Athens)/1994 and Ag.Stefanos prison (Patras)/ 1995 (4)	Korydallos prison (Athens) 1995	Various prisons In Greece/ 1996	Various prisons In Greece/ 1997-1998
Sample N	IDUs 191	Drug users 544	Prisoners 1 183	Prisoners 2 197	Prisoners 1 700
Metho-dology	Blood samples/ linked questionnaires	Blood samples/ linked questionnaires	Blood samples/ linked questionnaires	Blood samples	Blood samples
anti-HIV-1, n(%)	1 (0.54%)	1 (0.19%)	13 (1.10%)	3 (0.14%)	0 (0%)
anti-HCV, n(%)	147 (84.0%)	310 (58.2%)	325 (27.5%)	273 (12.4%)	251 (14.8%)
HbcAb, n(%)	80 (61.5%)	306 (57.6%)	575 (48.7%)	459 (20.9%)	734 (43.2%)
HbsAg, n(%)	ND	34 (6.5%)	89 (7.5%)	ND	184 (10.8%)
anti-HDV, n(%)	ND	12 (2.3%)	ND	ND	ND

2. Prison policies and prison realities

The Correctional Code of 1989 provides that prisoners should be examined by the prison physician on admission (or the day after their admission in prison at the latest). The official policy is to offer HIV and hepatitis B and C testing on a voluntary basis after counselling. The test results are recorded on the prisoners' health card that accompanies them in their transfers to other prisons. The above-mentioned are not always implemented because a) in nineteen out of twenty-eight prisons there is no full-time physician and as a result prisoners are examined when the physician visits the prison and b) some local hospitals cannot provide the serological testing needed. Although the official policy is to systematically offer a HIV test, the screening policy is heterogeneous; in some prisons HIV testing is offered systematically, elsewhere it is targeted at high risk groups and in other prisons it is impossible to implement. The HIV testing is offered by the prison physician, is voluntary and the rate of compliance is about 80%. Pre- and post-counselling is offered systematically.

At present, male inmates that are found to be HIV infected are transferred to the prison hospital where better living conditions and medical care are provided. Female HIV-positive prisoners stay in single cell accommodation in their prison without other restrictions except that they cannot work in posts related to food (this applies also for prisoners who are positive for hepatitis C and B markers). Medical treatment is administered to HIV infected prisoners as to HIV-positive patients in the community.

3. Details on other topics

Needle-exchange programmes are not available in Greek prisons. Bleach is provided in almost all prisons and an illustrated brochure about AIDS in prison is distributed to all inmates. On admission, a hygiene kit containing a shaving set (razors, shaving foam, soap, cotton etc.) is given to all prisoners. Since 1 January 1998 the WHO guidelines on AIDS in prison have been distributed to all prisons.

There are no substitution programmes offered in prison except if the prisoner had been following a methadone programme before entering prison and in that case he/she is allowed to continue. Imprisoned drug users receive psychotropic drugs. In Greek prisons, condoms and lubricants are not available. There is no possibility of heterosexual intercourse inside prison but this can occur during the short leaves (short leaves are available after one fifth of the sentence has been served).

4. Legal issues

Aids patients are released regardless of their sentence and of the time spent in prison except if they are recidivists. The first sentence given for drug trafficking can be substituted with an obligation to undergo drug treatment.

The sentencing of prisoners who deal with drugs inside prison is the same as when outside prison. Prisoners that are found in possession of substances are subject to disciplinary punishment and penal prosecution while the possession of injection equipment leads to disciplinary measures (isolation or/and privation of short leaves from prison or/and privation of visitors).

5. References

Quarterly edition of the Hellenic Centre for the Control of AIDS and STDs (September 1997) AIDS surveillance in Greece , no 4.

Papaevangelou G., Roumeliotou A., Stergiou G., Nestoridou A., Trichopoulou E. (1991) HIV infection in Greek intravenous users, European Journal of Epidemiology, 7, pp. 88-90.

Malliori M., Hatzakis A., Psichogiou M., Sipsa V., Touloumi G., Kokkevi A., Tassopoulos N., Stefanis C. (1996), Temporal changes in the prevalence of hepatotropic viruses and drug injection practices in Greek prisons, XI International Conference on AIDS, Vancouver, Vol. 1, pp. 353.

Malliori M, Sypsa V., Psichogiou G., Touloumi G., Skoutelis A., Tassopoulos N., Hatzakis A., Stefanis C. (1998), A survey of bloodborne viruses and associated risk behaviours in Greek prisons, Addiction, 93(2), pp. 243-251.

Drug Use by Prisoners
A review of the Irish Situation

Lucy Dillon

1 Introduction

At the second meeting of the Working Group on Drug Use In Prison (Strasbourg, 9 June 1999), it was agreed that each participating country would produce a review of their country's published and grey literature on the issue of drug use by prisoners. The five specific questions to be addressed were:

a. **Starting use**: Data concerning the initiation of individuals into drug use while in the prison setting [3.1].

b. **Changes in patterns of use**: Data concerning any changes in the volume and types of drugs being used by prisoners when in the prison setting. Both during incarceration and when compared to use prior to imprisonment [3.2].

c. **Changes in routes of administration/risk behaviour**: This is to consider data on changes between the various routes of administration with a particular focus on injecting behaviour. Particular focus on any data relating to changes in the patterns of risk behaviour that prisoners engage in due in the particular setting [3.3].

d. **Impact on on-going treatment**: This is to consider the effect imprisonment has had on the treatment which users receive. It will look at whether the programmes that individuals were involved in prior to incarceration were continued within the prison setting, and whether prison meant an initiation into treatment [3.4].

e. **Changes in motivation**: This more subjective focus is to consider data on the impact imprisonment has on an individual's motivation to engage in treatment [3.5].

At any one time, Ireland has a total of approximately 2 700 prisoners who are located in fifteen prisons nationwide (Allwright et al, 1999). The literature dealing with drug use among prisoners however, is extremely limited. A recent study carried out on the prevalence and risk of certain infectious diseases among Irish prisoners, was the first of its kind to look at health issues related to drug use on a national basis (Allwright et al, 1999). This study was carried out in nine prisons and involved 1 205 prisoners. For the purpose of the study, prisons were categorised according to expected prevalence rates for infection as high, medium or low. Five were classified as "high risk" prisons with four being referred to as "low risk". All five "high risk" prisons were in Dublin, the remainder were outside the capital. Four of the five "high risk" prisons were located within the Mountjoy prison complex.

It is essential to note that other available research has been carried out almost exclusively in one particular Dublin-based prison, namely Mountjoy. Where this is the case, data cannot be taken to be representative of Irish prisons as a whole. The nature of this prison as the main remand prison in Dublin means that there will be an over-concentration of drug users among this population. Prior to addressing the five questions laid out above, a brief overview will be given of the Irish literature available in this area. This literature has generally looked at the extent of drug use among prisoners, as opposed to either the nature of this drug use or whether it has persisted after incarceration.

2. Estimating drug use among Irish prisoners

2.1 Drug use and drug related convictions

Research on drug use among prisoners in Ireland continues to be very limited despite numerous anecdotal reports that drug misuse is presenting severe problems within the system. Existing research has generally looked at drug use only as part of a wider study. The main outcome of such research has been to give a rough estimate of the number of drug users within particular prison populations. Dependence on drug-related convictions as an indicator for these estimates has consistently been shown to obscure the true extent of drug use among prisoners. O'Mahony (1997(a)) argues that although there was a fifty-fold increase in the number of drug-related charges initiated by the Gardai (police) between 1965 and 1993 this continued to be a small proportion of the overall number of indictable crimes. In 1995 only 3 730 of an estimated 100 000 indictable crimes were drug related, the bulk of which were charges relating to the possession and supply of cannabis (O'Mahony, 1997 (a): 34). In 1995 under five per cent of the prison population was imprisoned on charges against the drug laws (Council of Europe, 1995). O'Mahony maintains that an analysis of drug-related convictions and committals largely underestimates the extent of the drug problem in Irish society and in particular the prison population. Further research carried out in this area confirms this view.

A study published in 1983 involved the use of a structured questionnaire that was administered to individuals in three different Dublin committal prisons, one of which was a juvenile detention centre. All participants had been identified as drug users who had "experience to the point of addiction, with drugs other than marijuana, alcohol and minor tranquillisers", (Gilmore et al, 1983: 23). The research found that in Mountjoy's main male prison only four of a sample of twenty-two drug users were serving sentences for drug related crimes. In the same study none of those interviewed in either the female section of Mountjoy (n=3) or in St. Patrick's Institution (n=9) were convicted of drug-related charges (Gilmore et al, 1983). O'Mahony carried out another study with a one-fifth systematic sample of the Mountjoy Male Prison population in 1996 (O'Mahony,

1997 (b)). Structured questionnaires were administered to 108 prisoners and the computerised criminal records of the sample were obtained from the central register of the Dublin Criminal Record system. O'Mahony found that while 66% of the total sample had used heroin only 6.9% were in prison for an offence against the Misuse of Drugs Acts (O'Mahony (b), 1997). Carmody et al's (1996) study of one hundred female prisoners in Mountjoy demonstrated a less distinctive pattern. Respondents were interviewed using a semi-structured questionnaire during their initial medical assessment.

Fifty-seven percent of their sample had been involved in drug use prior to imprisonment while 38% were in prison charged with drug related crimes. While among female prisoners there appears to be a stronger relationship between being a drug user and being convicted of a drug related crime, overall the use of drug related convictions as an indicator will underestimate the extent of drug use among prisoners.

2.2 Research estimating drug use among Irish prisoners

The studies discussed above highlighted the limitations of using drug related crimes as a basis for estimating drug use but they also provide a picture of the actual extent of drug use among certain prison populations. In their national study Allwright et al (1999) found that 52% of a national sample of prisoners reported a history of opiate use, with 43% reporting a history of injecting. In the "medium risk" prisons the rate of "ever injected" was 21% compared to 58% in the "high risk" prisons.

The remaining research has been limited to Mountjoy Prison, Dublin which cannot be considered representative of the overall prison population in relation to drug use. It is the main committal prison in the country and receives prisoners committed directly from the courts either under sentence or on remand. It has an average population of 650 prisoners on any one day. Due to the concentration of opiate use in the Dublin area (Moran et al, 1997) and evidence that approximately 66% of indictable crimes in the Dublin Metropolitan Area are committed by "known hard drug users", (Keogh, 1997) it is clear that Mountjoy will have a higher proportion of drug users in its population than other prisons. O'Mahony (1983; 1993; 1997) has carried out the most extensive research in this area. Over time his work has shown continued growth in the extent of drug use among this prison population.

The 1981 study by Gilmore and O'Mahony (1983) referred to earlier, carried out research on drug users in the committal prisons in Dublin. Three sampling sites were used: Mountjoy's male section (n=22), the female section (n=3) and the juvenile prison, St Patrick's (n=9). Admission of problematic drug use was a requirement of sample selection. Although the numbers were relatively small, drug use, in particular that of intravenous (IV) opiate use, was identified amongst those in the system as early as 1981. In Mountjoy's male prison twenty-two prisoners who admitted using drugs regularly prior to imprisonment were interviewed. On the basis of data gathered from prisoners, welfare and prison reports and verbal reports from officers working in the prison hospital, it was estimated that 8% of the convicted prison population were serious drug users. Sixteen of the twenty-two respondents were primarily opiate users with twelve citing heroin as the principal drug of use.

By the time the 1986 study was carried out the prevalence of drug use within this population had escalated dramatically (O'Mahony, 1993). O'Mahony carried out interviews with ninety-five prisoners using a structured questionnaire and accessed further information through the central criminal records register (Dublin Criminal Records). The proportion that reported long term, serious addiction problems had increased to 31% of the sample questioned. Fifty-nine percent of the sample reported having used cannabis at some stage and 37% having used additional illicit drugs, opiates being the most regularly cited.

The 1996 study was the most comprehensive to date and used a similar design to the 1986 study described above (O'Mahony, 1993; O'Mahony, 1997 (b)). It collected data on 108 male inmates to give a significant 'sociological and criminological profile' of Mountjoy's population (O'Mahony, 1997(b)). In relation to drug use it was found that the number reporting cannabis use had risen to 86% of the sample. The use of all other drugs had also risen significantly since the 1986 report with 77% stating that they had used drugs other than cannabis, 66% had used heroin. O'Mahony reports that while these prisoners were generally heroin users they did not use it exclusively and were overwhelmingly polydrug users. In addition, 63% of the overall sample were classified as having had a serious heroin dependency at some stage.

While most studies have been carried out in the male section of Mountjoy, a smaller number of studies have been carried out in the female wing of the prison. The first was carried out in 1989. This was a thesis for a Masters degree and remains unpublished (Monaghan, 1989). O'Mahony (1993) draws reference to it as a significant piece of research particularly in the absence of any other research with this group. Monaghan (1989) found that 53% of her sample of forty-seven women had abused illicit drugs, most being daily heroin users. This was found to be a significantly higher proportion than those using among the male population in O'Mahony's study (1986). A more recent study carried out by Carmody et al (1996) in the women's prison found that sixty percent of the sample had a history of illicit drug use. Ninety-five percent of these women reported heroin as their drug of use and 92% reported that they were using it on a daily basis at the time of committal.

While the data collected through these pieces of research are not directly comparable due to variations in methodology, they give a clear picture of an escalation of drug use among prisoners in at least one Irish prison. The presence of illicit drugs in Mountjoy has lead at least one commentator to conclude that the prison is "totally dominated by a drugs culture embodied in prisoners' attitudes, values and behaviours" (O'Mahony, 1997 (a), p42).

Table 1: Summary of Irish research findings

Year of fieldwork	Author (publication date)	Prison	Sample size	% Ever used opiates
1981	O'Mahony & Gilmore (1983)	Mountjoy: Male Section	22*	72* [8**]
1986	O'Mahony (1993)	Mountjoy: Male Section	95	32
1996	O'Mahony (1997)	Mountjoy: Male Section	108	66
1999	Allwright et al (1999)	National Survey	1 205	52
1989	Monaghan (unpublished)	Mountjoy: Female Section	34	31
1994	Carmody & McEvoy (1996)	Mountjoy: Female Section	100	57

*   Sample solely made up of prisoners that described themselves as "drug abusers"

**   This figure was an estimate based on data gathered from the sample (all of whom admitted drug abuse), welfare and prison records and prison hospital officers.

57

3. Drug use within the environment of Irish prisons

Irish studies demonstrate that in at least one of Ireland's prisons the proportion of individuals with a history of drug use has grown consistently over the last decade and a half. Most of these studies however have not considered the extent and nature of drug use by these prisoners *while* incarcerated. Two studies however, have looked at this issue, one on a national basis (Allwright et al, 1999), the other within one prison (O'Mahony, 1997 (b)). Rather than questioning respondents solely about their drug using habits prior to their imprisonment these studies have explored the extent to which prisoners used drugs *while in* prison. These are the principal sources of information for responses to the five questions laid out in *section 1* above.

3.1 Initiation into drug use

Initiation into illicit drug use among prisoners has not been explored in the context of Irish prisons. No data are available on the extent to which prisoners are initiated into their first ever drug use within the Irish prison system. As will be seen in later sections there is only evidence of initiation into new drugs of use or new routes of administration rather than any illicit drug use per se (Allwright (1999); O'Mahony's (1997 (b)).

3.2 Changes in patterns of use

"Changes in the patterns of use" has been taken to refer to the types of drugs used. O'Mahony found that 42% (n=45) of the total sample of 108 prisoners had used heroin while in prison serving their current sentence. This was 63% of those that had ever used heroin. Overall only eighteen of the sixty people with a history of intravenous drug use claimed *not* to have used heroin during their current sentence. O'Mahony (1997(b)) highlights however, that most of this group had been incarcerated for a short time at the time of interview, eleven for a month or less and five for a week or less. Consequently these respondents may not yet have been presented with the opportunity to use drugs. Of those that were convicted and had been imprisoned for a minimum of three months 56% (n=29) were using heroin in prison. Within the total group (n=45) that reported using while in prison twenty-three reported either daily use or use several times a week, sixteen said they used about once a week and six less than once a week or only very occasionally. Lack of access to drugs appeared to be the main reason for a lower frequency of use. It was found that access to heroin varied between locations within the prison. Some prisoners reported easy access to supplies while others reporting more sporadic availability. In general drugs became available either through visits or from other prisoners. Overall, entering prison did not mean a cessation of drug use.

Six prisoners in O'Mahony's (1997 (b)) sample reported that their first ever experience of heroin had been within the prison setting. One other reported that while he had used heroin prior to imprisonment it had been while serving a previous sentence that he had become dependent. There was also some anecdotal evidence suggesting that as a result of more stringent searching after visits, cannabis had become more difficult to access within the prison. It was suggested that its absence meant some prisoners had resorted to heroin use. The findings from this piece of research that some prisoners are initiated into heroin use while in prison, and the anecdotal evidence that a more widespread shift toward heroin use may be occurring, presents a serious challenge to those working in this area.

3.3 Changes in routes of administration/risk behaviour

Allwright et al's (1999) study focused on the risk behaviours engaged in by prisoners in relation to the spread of Hepatitis B, Hepatitis C and HIV. One fifth (104/506) of those reporting a history of injecting drug use said that they had first begun injecting drugs while in prison. In considering the risk behaviours engaged in by these prisoners it was found that injecting drug users were more likely to share injecting equipment while in prison than outside this setting. Allwright et al (1999) found that 58% of injecting drug users said they had shared all injecting equipment (i.e. needles, syringes, filters, spoons) while in prison, compared to 37% that reported sharing in the month prior to being incarcerated. This was found to have serious repercussions on the health status of prisoners. Of those that had shared equipment inside the prison, 89.1% had tested positive for Hepatitis C, compared to 62.2% of those who had not shared in prison.

O'Mahony's (1997 (b)) study of prisoners in Mountjoy prison found that 42% (n=45) of a total sample of 108 prisoners had used heroin while in prison serving their current sentence. Thirty-seven of these had engaged in intravenous drug use. One-sixth of those reporting a history of drug use had tested positive for HIV while a quarter had never been tested. In addition, half of these drug users said that they had tested positive for at least one form of hepatitis. O'Mahony described as 'alarming' (O'Mahony, 1997: p. 107) the finding that of those who reported having tested positive for HIV, 60% had engaged in needle sharing since finding out. An earlier study based on data gathered between 1987 and 1991 found that 168 known HIV positive prisoners had spent time in Mountjoy during the same period. A study of a sub-sample of these, selected on a random basis, found that 94% had engaged in drug use within the prison, suggesting a potential spread of HIV to uninfected prisoners (Murphy et al, 1992).

The report of Mountjoy's visiting committee also offers evidence that prisoners continue to engage in intravenous drug use while in prison. In their interim report for 1998 they emphasise the continuation of overcrowding and drug use as the key problems in the prison. Security measures have been increased in relation to drug use in the prison and continue to highlight the extent of drug use within the prison setting. As a result of increased searches from 1 January until 6 July 1998 there were 139 seizures of drugs within the prison. In addition there were 137 cases of prisoners who were found in possession of a syringe and 61 "prohibited articles", such as the plunger of a syringe found and confiscated, (Mountjoy Visiting Committee, 1998). The confiscation of such articles and the on-going intravenous drug use of some prisoners may suggest increased risk behaviour.

Despite the potential for the spread of HIV or hepatitis among intravenous drug users in the prison setting there are no harm reduction strategies in place in the Irish prison system (O'Brien et al, 1997). An award winning booklet and video containing information for prisoners on HIV discrimination, infection and prevention have been produced and are supposedly available to all prisoners (Weilandt et al 1998). However a report evaluating services in this field which involved focus group interviews with prisoners and former prisoners, found that these HIV positive individuals had not seen either of these materials (O'Brien et al, 1997).

3.4 Impact on On-going Treatment

In a 1994 document, the Department of Justice clearly stated equivalence of care and provision for the continuity of care as among the objectives of the prison medical services in Ireland:

> "To provide primary health care (prevention, treatment and health rehabilitation) to offenders of at least an equivalent standard to that available to citizens in the general community; this involves as a minimum an adequate reception, medical assessment and examination, through-care while in prison and making appropriate arrangements for the continuation of health care following release."
> *(Department of Justice, 1994)*

This stance was reiterated in a 1999 document concerned with treatment provision in the prison setting (Department of Justice, Equality and Law Reform, 1999). The care of drug users in the community falls within the remit of the Department of Health and Children whereas in the prison setting it is the responsibility of the Department of Justice, Equality and Law Reform. This situation creates inherent problems for the continuity of care of drug users. Despite on-going commitments, the principle of equivalence does not prevail within the Irish prison system in its care of drug users.

Despite current expansions, the services available to Irish prisoners remain limited and have been overwhelmingly based on short-term detoxification and abstinence programmes. As with other aspects of drug use in Irish prisons the focus of literature concerning services has been on Mountjoy prison. Recent changes in Mountjoy have seen a limited expansion of the services available to prisoners as reported in the interim report of the Visiting Committee, (Mountjoy Visiting Committee, 1998). Firstly, there is a standard detoxification programme of fourteen days, which is offered to prisoners on committal if they are found to test positive for opiates. Prisoners that may have been stable on methadone in the community are generally detoxified upon incarceration. Melleril (25mgs) is also offered for the first seven nights during detoxification. Secondly, there is a methadone maintenance programme that offers a limited number of places.

There are approximately twenty prisoners on this programme at any one time. Consultant psychiatrists form the Drug Treatment Centre, Trinity Court supervise the programme with a prison doctor. Daily urine samples are taken from the prisoners to discourage illicit drug use. Thirdly, there is a seven-week rehabilitation programme based in the Medical Unit that caters for nine prisoners at a time. A tailor-made detoxification programme is offered in the first week, followed by an intensive six-week therapy programme. Participants who have managed to remain drug free are then transferred to the Training Unit which is a drug free environment. It is important to note that these services are all available in the *male* section of the prison. Carmody et al (1996) found that thirty-one of a sample of fifty-seven female prisoners with a history of heroin use, were on a methadone maintenance programme at the time of committal. There are however no services within this women's prison to continue these women's maintenance on methadone.

Crowley (1998) provided a medical review of the seven-week rehabilitation programme in Mountjoy. His review of the service cited positive results for the programme. However he highlighted the need for an expansion of the programme both in terms of places and the services offered. In addition he highlighted the detrimental effects of being returned to the main prison i.e. to a "less secure and regulated environment in terms of illicit drugs availability" (Crowley, 1998).

While epidemiological data is gathered on those receiving treatment in the general community in Ireland such a system is only being established in the prison context at present. Within the Irish prison system there is no systematic collection of epidemiological data either on those prisoners with a history of drug use or those attending treatment. As a consequence it is not possible to give an overview of the numbers engaging in treatment within the Irish prison system. A study examining the feasibility of the inclusion of prisons in the National Drug Treatment Reporting System produced positive findings (Duff et al, 1999). The recommendations of the study are being implemented with the co-operation of the relevant individuals and authorities. This will lead to sound epidemiological information on drug users in treatment within prison, in the near future.

3.5 Changes in Motivation to Attend Treatment

No research has been carried out to examine changes in prisoners' motivation to attend treatment upon imprisonment. While a number of prisoners may be motivated to seek treatment the lack of services may be seen as prohibiting them to do so.

4. Conclusion

Drug use among prisoners is an on-going issue facing the Irish prison system. There is a significant body of evidence to show that prisoners continue to engage in drug use while in prison, (O'Mahony, 1997 (b); Cork Visiting Committee, 1997; Mountjoy Prison Visiting Committee, 1998; Allwright et al, 1999). The nature of drug use among Irish prisoners has been found to change while incarcerated, both in terms of the drugs they use and the route of administration they are used by (Allwright et al, 1999; O'Mahony, 1997 (b)). These changes often involve increased health risks, particularly in relation to intravenous drug use and the spread of HIV and other infectious diseases among Irish prisoners (Allwright et al, 1999). While the availability of services for drug users is expanding in the Irish prison system there is an on-going gap in both the continuity and equivalence of care within this system. One contributing factor to this is that the care of drug users in the community falls within the remit of the Department of Health and Children while within prison it is the responsibility of the Department of Justice, Equality and Law Reform.

5. References

Allwright, Shane, Barry, Joseph, Bradley, Fiona, Long, Jean, Thornton, Lelia, (1999) *Hepatitis B, Hepatitis C and HIV in Irish Prisoners: Prevalence and Risk*, Department of Justice Equality and Law Reform, Government Publications

Carmody, Patricia, McEvoy, Mel (January 1996) *A Study of Irish Female Prisoners*, Government Publications

Council of Europe, (1995) *Council of Europe Annual Penal Statistics (SPACE)*

Crowley, Des (1998) *A Twelve Monthly Medical review of the Drug Treatment and Detoxification Unit at Mountjoy Prison* in Working group on a Courts Commission, Fifth Report, Drug Courts, February, 1998

Department of Justice (1994) *The Management of Offenders: A Five Year Plan*, Government Publications

Department of Justice, Equality and Law Reform (1999), *Drug Misuse and Drug Treatment in the Prison System, Department of Justice, Equality and Law Reform*

Duff, Petrina, Moran, Rosalyn and O'Brien, Mary, 1999, *The Feasibility of the Inclusion of General Practitioners and Prisons in the National Drug Treatment reporting System*, Health Research Board

EMCDDA, (1998) *Annual report on the State of the Drugs Problem in the European Union, 1998*, Office for Official Publications of the European Communities, Luxembourg

Gilmore, T, O'Mahony, Paul (1983) *Drug Abusers in the Dublin Committal Prisons: A Survey*, Stationery Office

Government Strategy to Prevent Drug Misuse, May 1991, Department of Health

Keogh, Eamonn, (1997) *Illicit Drug Use and Related Criminal activity in the Dublin Metropolitan Area*, Garda Research Unit

Ministerial Task Force, (1997), *The Second Report of the Ministerial Task Force on Measures to Reduce the Demand for Drugs*, May 1997

Monaghan, M. (1989) *A Survey of Women in an Irish Prison*, University College Dublin: M.Psych.Sc. dissertation, cited in O'Mahony, Paul (1993) Crime and Punishment in Ireland, The Round Hall Press

Moran, Rosalyn, O'Brien, Mary and Duff, Petrina (1997) *Treated Drug Misuse in Ireland*, Health Research Board

Mountjoy Prison Visiting Committee (1998), *Mountjoy Prison Visiting Committee Interim Report, April 1998-October 1998*, Department of Justice [unpublished]

Murphy, M., Gaffney, K, O'Carey, O, Dolley, E, Mulcahy, F, (1992) *The Impact of HIV Disease on an Irish Prison Population,* International Journal of STD & AIDS, 3: pp426-429

National Steering Group on Deaths in Prisons (1999), *Report of the National Steering group on Deaths in Prisons*, Department of Justice

O'Brien, Oonagh & Stevens, Alex, (1997), *A Question of Equivalence: A Report on the Implementation of International Guidelines on HIV/AIDS in Prisons of the European Union*, Cranstoun Drug Services, London

O'Mahony, Paul (1993) *Crime and Punishment in Ireland*, The Round Hall Press

O'Mahony, Paul (1997 (a)) *The Drugs Culture and Drug Rehabilitation within the Prison System*, in 'The Management of the Drug Offender in Prison and on Probation', published seminar papers, IMPACT

O'Mahony, Paul (June 1997 (b)) *Mountjoy Prisoners: A Sociological and Criminological Profile*, Department of Justice

St.Patrick's Visiting Committee, (1997) *St. Patrick's Institution Visiting Committee Annual Report for 1997*, Department of Justice [unpublished]

Weilandt, Caren, Rotily, Michel, *Annual Report of the European Network on HIV/AIDS and Hepatitis Prevention in Prisons*, May 1998

Malta Report

Richard Muscat

1. Contributions

This report is partly based on the evidence presented at a Seminar on Drug Use in Prison held on the 30 June 1999 at the local drug agency, Sedqa.

In part, it also based on a series of discussions held with Mr. Anthony Schembri, the Assistant Manager of Education and Rehabilitation, at the correctional facility in Malta who in turn is responsible for the day to day running of the premises.

It also the result of a long interview held with Dr. John Zammit Montebello, Director of the drug free wing at the correctional facility here in Malta.

Finally, the input of Dr. Maria Sciberras, a member of the Prison Board, is included as a result of her expertise in the drug field, her specific role in the introduction of urine testing at the facility and the inception of a juvenile wing.

2. Background

Approval by the Permanent Correspondents of the Pompidou Group for the Drug Use in Prison project was first sought in 1997. The project in its entirety was put forward by Ms. Luisa Machado Rodrigues (P-PG/Epid (98) 16 rev) and approval was given at the 40th meeting of the Permanent Correspondents (October 1997). Since that time, two informal meetings of the group have taken place, one in Lisbon in July 1998, and the other at the first Project Group Meeting in the field of Epidemiology (30 November-1 December 1998). To date there have also been two working group meetings; the first took place in Paris in March 1999, a report of which was forwarded to all interested parties by Ms. Luisa Machado Rodrigues (P-PG/Epid (99) 9 E). The major outcome of that meeting was that a key list of words or guidelines be provided to each member by the co-ordinator for discussion at the second working group meeting (P-PG/Epid (99) 12 E). This meeting was held in Strasbourg in June 1999 and following long but positive discussions it was agreed by the group that each member produce a summary of Drug use in Prison of their respective countries along the following guidelines (P-PG/Epid (99) 14 E). The key question to be addressed was that of: *"What impact does prison have on drug use?"*

In attempting to answer this question, each document incorporated the following elements.

-    Section 1 - basic information from the Guidelines.

- Do inmates start or stop drug use while in prison?

- Are there any changes in patterns of use from the point of view of switching from cannabis to heroin or vice-versa? In addition, are there any changes in frequency, quantity and volume of drugs used while in prison?

- In the case of drug use are there any changes in the route of administration and what effects does prison have on the individual in the case of sharing equipment?

- Does the fact that an individual has been sent to prison result in any changes in ongoing treatment?

- Finally, is there any evidence that prison influences the individual's motivation to stop drug use?

3. Introduction

In the field of jurisdiction, Malta has now acceded to the 1988 United Nations Convention against Illicit Trafficking in Narcotic Drugs and Psychotropic Substances. A bill has now been passed through parliament to include psychotropics as well as the conventional narcotics. In 1994, The Prevention of Money Laundering Act was passed and in the same year the Dangerous Drugs Ordinance was also amended to include coerced treatment and a more complete definition of a trafficking offence. This year, the law on trafficking was again amended to resolve the apparent differences between bringing in drugs for personal use and that for trafficking. These changes in the law by successive governments in which stiffer penalties for drug traffickers were introduced, along with the freezing and forfeiture of assets, are a major attempt to limit illicit drug trafficking.

In Malta, it is a criminal offence to be in possession of any amount of the illicit substances whether for personal use or for that matter to traffic in these drugs. The figures for arrests by the police for possession or trafficking total 545. To date, 203 cases have come to court in which sixty (fifty-four male and six female) have been charged for trafficking offences. The courts have also resolved 143 cases of possession, which implies personal use. In these cases of possession it is not unusual for the courts to hand down a suspended sentence if the case in question relates to a first time offender provided that the individual seeks helps from the local drug agencies. A problem that seems to occur with such a procedure is that a number of these cases fall foul of the law during this period on a number of occasions that are sometimes drug related and sometimes not. It is not unusual then for an individual to have a number of pending cases that take a considerable time to come to court but by the time they do a person may be in dire straits as regards his sentence and escalating drug habit. Thus, in all probability, the type of individual that the correctional facility now receives is one that has a catalogue of problems.

Those individuals that are not granted bail are sent to prison pending their court case which may take some time. In July 1999, a total of 240 inmates, seventy-one of these were awaiting trial. Due to this fact they are not considered by the authorities for any drug programmes that are currently within operation at the institution.

There is only one prison on the Island, and at any one time it can cater for some 300 individuals. As stated above, during the month of July the number of inmates totalled 240, of these 236 were male and four female. Three prisoners are serving life sentences, twenty-four have sentences for greater than 10 years, ninety-one prisoners are serving time for between 2 and 10 years and fifty-one prisoners have been sentenced for 2 years or less. Of the twenty-four serving time for longer than 10 years, thirteen have been incarcerated for drug related offences and none of them have been previously registered at the Detoxification Unit. Forty-five of the nintey-one inmates serving between 2 and 10 years are doing time for drug related offences, six of which have a previous history of drug use. Finally, of the fifty-one serving time for less than 2 years, seventeen inmates are there because of a drug related offence, six of whom were registered at the Detoxification Unit. To summarise, out of a total of 169 sentenced inmates, seventy-five sentences are related to drug offences while the other ninety-four are not. In relation to those awaiting trial who total seventy-one, thirty-seven are awaiting trial on drug related offences while thirty-four are not.

The staff compliment at this single facility include: 1 Director, 4 Assistant Managers, 4 Supervisors, 17 Senior Correction Officers, 161 Correction Officers. With regard to health and other professionals the prison is served by: 5 General Practitioners on a part-time basis, 1 Psychiatrist on a part-time basis, 1 Dentist on a part-time basis, 1 Pharmacist on a part-time basis, 2 Education Co-ordinators on a full-time basis, 1 Psychologist on a full-time basis, 5 Probation officers on a full-time basis.

The Drug Rehabilitation Unit consists of the following staff: 1 General Practitioner on a full-time basis, 2 Senior Correction Officers on a full-time basis, 6 Correction Officers on a full-time basis, 1 Psychologist on a part-time basis, 1 Educationalist on a part-time basis, 1 Therapist on a part-time basis.

The major changes that have taken place within the prison confines have been related to the staff compliment which are due in the main to the following reasons:

1.   Provision of a 24 hour GP service.

2.   Health screening for HIV, hepatitis C and tuberculosis on entry and every six months.

3.   Classification of inmates using the following criteria:

   a.   Maximum security.
   b.   Juvenile (Drug Free).
   c.   Female.
   d.   Drug Free Wing.

The Juvenile Wing has just come into operation and is considered to be a drug free wing, catering for those of twenty-one years of age or under. In July, thirteen inmates were housed in this facility, two of which were serving sentences for drug law offences, while six had a previous history of drug use.

The Drug Free Wing has been in operation since October 1995 and has a maximum capacity of twenty residents at any one time but it is optimally operated at the level of fourteen residents. Inclusion of inmates to this wing is strictly determined by length of sentence; only those serving between six months and two years are given the option to be housed in this wing.

4.   Do inmates stop or start drug use in prison?

It is generally assumed that within the confines of a prison drug use ceases. However, from epidemiological data from around Europe (*EMCDDA Annual Report*) and more specifically prevalence studies, it would appear that drug use does go on in prison. The results of these studies do not give any information as to whether it would have been any greater or lesser if the individuals had been outside these confines and as such do not provide a baseline from which to establish if the former or latter occurs. Of those that satisfy the inclusion criteria to be housed in the drug free wing here in Malta, it is estimated that 90% do not avail themselves of this opportunity single handedly. Most inmates have difficulties in making such decisions following incarceration and those that do, normally opt for such, thinking that they will be better off in this type of structure without taking into account their drug problem. Nowadays, the team running the wing prepares the inmates for what to expect in such a facility, commonly known as a pre-contemplative stage, which takes some three months. Such a strategy has reduced the number of inmates opting to go back to the main prison following some weeks on the wing.

It is estimated that of the prison population of 240, 5% or twelve individuals first make use of drugs while serving their sentence. It is also assumed that these individuals are mainly first time offenders.

To summarise, it would appear that the prison confines do not provide the necessary backdrop from which an individual may decide to stop using drugs. On the contrary, it would appear to facilitate the initiation of drug use in those individuals that did not do so in open society here in Malta.

5. Are there any changes in patterns of drug use?

The finding that drug use still goes on prison is supported by random urine testing (15% of the total prison population) that occurs on a monthly basis in the correctional facility in Malta. The results of which also point to no switch from what are termed hard to soft drugs. Mandatory urine testing of maximum security inmates also supports the findings with the random test system carried out on the prison population as a whole.

However, frequency, quantity and volume of drug use would appear to be reduced if one relies on the results of random and mandatory urine testing. Over the past three months of a total of some 100 random tests, one was positive for cannabis and the other was positive for heroin. In the case of mandatory testing, nine of a total of fifteen were positive for heroin and cocaine in a maximum security wing.

To summarise, there is no evidence from the facility in question for a switch from hard to soft drugs or vice-versa. However, it would appear that the frequency, quantity and volume of drugs is reduced in the local prison settings.

6. Any changes in the route of administration?

It would appear that the inmates housed in the local prison do not resort to injection which may have been the preferred route on the outside. This is largely owing to the size of the facility. Most of the inmates are in daily contact with the correctional officers and are well known which makes it rather difficult for them to hide track marks. Furthermore, it is customary to carry out searches of the cells that further prevents the use of such materials. In addition, HIV tests are implemented on entry and every six months and to date no positive tests have resulted. With regard to hepatitis C, tests are also conducted on entry and every six months. However, it would appear that approximately 33% of the prison population have tested positive. Due to the length of the incubation period, one cannot determine whether it was contracted inside the prison or prior to admission. Overall, it would appear that prison has a positive effect on the problems associated with injecting and the risk associated with the sharing of injecting equipment.

To summarise, the evidence available in relation to route of administration would seem to support the fact for a positive change from injecting and the associated risks to other less risky routes of administration.

7. Any changes in ongoing treatment?

No methadone administration is carried out within the prison facility here in Malta following a number of problems that arose with the use of such a procedure. However, on entry all individuals are required on medical grounds to provide a urine sample for drug analysis. Those individuals receiving any form of treatment for their drug condition are given the option of spending 24 hours at the local psychiatric hospital for observation following which a recommendation is made by the psychiatrist as to whether or not the individual is to receive any further treatment. In the likelihood that the individual is to continue methadone treatment, the said inmate is taken daily to the Detoxification Unit outside the grounds of the general hospital. The numbers of inmates opting for this form of assessment is limited, some two-three in the last month. This would in turn suggest that they would rather stop treatment than undergo such formalities.

To summarise, the likelihood of an inmate continuing methadone treatment inside prison is a rare occurrence.

8. Does prison influence the desire to stop drug use?

From what has been ascertained above, it would seem to suggest in the first instance that the prison confines do not have a positive effect on the individuals desire to stop drug use. In some individuals it may indeed have the opposite effect, i.e. those that first use drugs in prison and the discontinuation of methadone treatment. However, as was also pointed out, those finally arriving at the prison gates have compounded their situation for a number of reasons and are not in the right frame of mind to even consider such drastic measures as stopping their drug use. In addition, of those that do make an attempt to get onto the drug free wing following a pre-contemplative stage, it has been found that 60% of this cohort have serious psychiatric problems and should be in hospital not prison. A further number have psychological problems.

To summarise, prison on the whole has a deleterious effect on the desire of the individual to stop drug use. However, the situation may not be as straightforward as it would first appear. There is documented and circumstantial evidence to support the notion that in a number of individuals the problem of drug use per se obfuscates other more serious underlying phenomena.

9. Conclusions

From the point of view of health in prisons, these confines should provide the opportunity for those with a drug problem to be treated in a like manner to those at large. On the surface however, the opposite occurs. Individuals are more likely to start drug use in prison, those on treatment are less likely to receive it and finally the place does not motivate one to stop drug use. However, there are certain judicial circumstances that result in the individual being incarcerated in the first place. Here in Malta, the fact that an individual can be left pending with a court case for up to three years is problematic as this normally results in:

a. Spending time in prison awaiting trial but without access to drug programmes.

b. Further offences while on bail, that finally results in a substantial sentence that again precludes the individual from participating on a drug programme while in prison.

It would be more appropriate if Drug Courts were established in which individuals were promptly dealt with by the said institution. In theory, they would have the capability to resolve the problems in question by having at their disposal a team of experts to assess the individual being charged. This may in turn distinguish between the occasional user and those that are in need of professional attention.

One might also wish to consider the availability of some form of drug intervention for those serving sentences of longer than two years. At present, it is only those inmates serving time for two years or less that may opt for such intervention.

10. References

Luisa Machado-Rodrigues Drug use by Prisoners, Project Proposal, (P-PG/Epid (98) 16 rev E).

Drug use by Prisoners, 1st working group meeting, Paris, March 1999. Summary of the discussions (P-PG/Epid (99) 9 E).

Richard Muscat Drug use by Prisoners, Guidelines (P-PG/Epid (99) 12 E).

Drug use by Prisoners, 2nd working group meeting (Strasbourg, June 1999). Summary of the discussions. P-PG/Epid (99) 14 E.

Dutch report

Dr van Alem, Dr Wisselink, Dr Groen

1. Introduction

Law enforcement has been a dominant theme in tackling drug use, traffic and trade and in finding ways to bring users into treatment, either during the pre-trial phase or in detention. Within the chain of law enforcement options used, prison is a last resort. The iatrogenic effect of a prison sentence has been documented extensively in fiction as well as in epidemiological and criminological studies (see Tulkens, 1988) On the other hand, it is also documented that a sentence or a confrontation with the law can have a beneficial effect (Biernacki, 1986).

In the Netherlands, drug use and prison emerged as a theme in policy as well as research in the mid-seventies (van Alem et.al. 1989). It lasted however until the nineties before the first "circumstantial evidence" became available on the effects of specific treatment modalities and options within the law enforcement chain (van den Hurk, 1998; Jongerius et.al. 1997; Bieleman et.al. 1999; Bulten, 1998). These quasi-experimental and observational studies mark a shift in attention, as well as the various white papers published by the Dutch government (Dwang en drang, 1993).

First, the aims of this project will be described. After that, an extensive picture will be drawn of the structure and changes in Dutch drug policy, more specifically the Dutch penitentiary drug policy, an outline of the correctional system, the options currently available for drug users in the criminal justice system, their structure, capacity and the way programmes are operated.

2. Aims

This report focuses on the prison as a lever for change; change in drug use, an opportunity to start treatment or just a time out facility to refuel for streetlife (Timmermans, 1998). The focus of the report will be on the total population processed by the Dutch criminal justice system, ie. (identified and non-identified) drug users entering the prison system as well as non-drug users. The report is written in the framework of the project "Drug Use in Prison" of the Pompidou Group of the Council of Europe.

Five questions will be addressed as to whether changes are observed in the following:

- starting/continuing drug use?
- patterns of use? (frequency, quantity, setting)

- routes of administration (risk behaviour)?
- patterns of treatment (continuation, start, disruption) ?
- motivation to stop drug use or to enter treatment?

3. Method

The report is based on three main sources: research and policy documents (1), interviews with key figures (2) and data available from criminal justice system information systems (3). Interviews have been held with a number of key representatives (professionals working in the field, officials of the Ministry of Justice and the Health Inspectorate of the Correctional Institutions). They also recieved a letter with the outlines of this project and the main questions to be addressed; annex 1 contains a list with those interviewed. The project took place in July and August 1999.

4. Dutch drug policy

One of the tenets of Dutch policy on drug (and alcohol) use has been the public health approach towards the problem. Both problems warrant public health interventions because of the public safety aspects of both alcohol and drugs. In the field of drug use one could state that the Dutch government's *harm-reduction approach* has had remarkable political impact. The basic assumption of this approach is that, by offering low-threshold methadone programmes, implementing needle exchange programmes and distributing condoms, the secondary consequences of drug abuse can be controlled. Secondary consequences being disease transmission, crime, illegal drug trading etc. Factors, among others, which can also have a negative impact on public safety (Veiligheidsrapportage BIZA, 1998). Nationally and internationally remarkable results are being attributed to this approach. Assuming that drug related deaths are a valid indicator for this approach, the Netherlands has had a comparatively low mortality figure and a relatively low number of HIV infected drug users (CBS, 1999).

Another term specifically coined by the Dutch is the "gedoogbeleid" - a policy of tolerance which tries to find *"the third way"*(!) between prohibition and legalisation. Coffee shops are allowed and fit into a tradition were Dutch administrators try to offer space for deviant behaviour within a controlled context. The legitimacy of Dutch drug policy is heavily influenced by the public health approach and rhetoric. It aims to keep in touch with drug users either by offering low threshold treatment or by creating localities where those who want to experiment with soft drugs can do so in a controlled fashion. This last approach is based on the "division of markets", another tenet of Dutch drug policy.

All indicators of illicit drug dependence have continued to climb over the past two decades, showing no sign of reversal. Compared to other European states, the number of addicts per 10 000 inhabitants is average. In recent years the number of clients with a primary alcohol problem has been decreasing; contrary to illegal drugs like opiates and cocaine. The total number of clients has been increasing slowly since the beginning of the nineties (LADIS Kerncijfers 1997).

Despite its successes, there have been a number of developments casting doubt on the impact of Dutch policy. Increasingly citizens have organised themselves in the battle against drug trading and dealing. Moreover, the Dutch criminal justice system has been pervasively influenced by drugs. About 50-60% of the detainees are drug misusers. Currently it is estimated that so called "criminal hard drug users" commit 70 000 crimes per annum; which is about 10% of all crimes committed annually (Verslavingszorg herijkt, 1999).

Increasingly political pressure grew from outside. As European member states started to open their borders (as a result of the Schengen treaty) criticism grew as to the liberal aspects of Dutch drug policy. On the other hand, other countries acknowledged the added value of methadone programmes as instruments of coming into contact and monitoring at risk populations.

Against this picture, a new drug policy originated which on the one hand facilitated the development of a treatment orientation within correctional institutions while on the other hand more (treatment) options were introduced which gave drug users in prison (arrest, custody or sentenced) an option to enter, or become motivated to enter treatment. These options can be described by a number of "either/or" options (ie. prison sentence or treatment) or "and/and"options where treatment is a condition and part of the sentence. The main theme of the white paper "continuity and change" (VWS, 1995) was the continuation of the pragmatic approach, but only if additional changes were made at those points where the side effects of Dutch drug policy outweighed the benefits.

5. Outline of the Dutch correctional system [1]

During the last eight years, the formal capacity of the penal institutions has risen from 7 677 in 1990 to 12 553 in 1998 - an increase of about 40%. Until the mid eighties, the Netherlands had one of the lowest number of cells per 100 000 of the population and in 1990 51.55 cells per 100 000 inhabitants). In 1996 – when there were 75 cells per 100 000 of the population, it belonged to the lower band of the European average (about 84/100 000). The estimated

---

[1]   This section is mainly based on documentation provided by the National Agency of Correctional Institutions (DJI) of the Dutch Ministry of Justice (Prisons, 1999; Fact and Figures, 1999)

expenditure of the Ministry of Justice for correctional institutions is about 23% of its total expenditure.

Table 1 gives an overview of the formal capacity of the Dutch prison system according to the various types of modalities. Only 4% of the total prison population are female.

Table 1: Key figures (1998)

Detention modality	Capacity	Target group	Aim
Detention centre	6 653	All those held in custody and waiting for placement in a prison	Remand in custody
Closed prisons	2 373	All inmates	Executing sentence
Half-open prisons	340	Inmates with 1.5 years left	Preparation for re-entry in society
Open prisons	216	Inmates with maximum remaining sentence of 5 months	Preparation for re-entry in society; only evening/ night stay
Other types	2 971	ie. Juveniles, arrestees, day detention.	
Total capacity	12 553		

In 1997, there was a total of 11 770 detainees (see table 2) within the different detention centres. In 1997, about 46% of all the detainees were between 15-29 years. About 50% are Dutch and over 30% come from either South America or Africa.

Table 2: Key figures

	1996	1997
Total population in detention centre	11 931 34% on remand 66% in prison	11 770 35% on remand 65% in prison
Total population in contact during the year	38 756	40 836
Number of days per detainee	105	105

(*Source: CBS, 1999*)

Custodial sentences are enforced according to the (new) Penitentiary Institutions Act, which entered into force in 1999. The act governs the placement of inmates in institutions. The custodial system has different categories of detention to age, gender, psychiatric disability, specific forensic institutes and capacity specifically meant for drug users in prison. The act also offers a framework for regulations permitting infringement on certain rights. The proper enforcement of these rules is monitored by the Central Council for the Application of Criminal Law.

In the thirty-nine detention centres in the Netherlands, there is about one general practitioner for every 300 detainees (and a total of eighty general practitioners) and one nurse for every forty detainees. Most centres employ a psychologist (in total sixty-five) while a psychiatrist (fifty in total) is on call.

6. Drug users and the criminal justice system: Entry and exit options

Before and during contact with the criminal justice system there are a number of *filters* within that system; these filters are based on the legal rules and phases as well as priority setting by law enforcement agencies. In a great number of countries police and prosecution are formally obliged to bring to court any crime that is detected (ie. the legality principle). The Netherlands on the contrary has committed itself to the "expediency principle" which allows discretionary powers to the police and the prosecution. Since a number of years there are specific guidelines on how to deal with certain cases under specified conditions (Silvis, 1994).

Thus the selection of drug users finally entering the prison system, and receiving a prison sentence and accepting some form of treatment is a selective group, because in the earlier phases a process of "cream skimming" has taken place ie. eligible and motivated users leave as early as possible.

The number of detainees under suspicion or sentenced under the Opium Act cannot be used as an indicator to estimate the size of the population because of these filters. Most of these sentences deal with traffic and trade offenders.

Since the beginning of the nineties, an extensive framework has grown which aims at getting drug users entering the criminal justice system into treatment. This shift in approach was first reflected in a government paper in the late eighties (Dwang en drang, 1988). Since then, the number of options to deal with drug users has increased. The central theme underlying this policy in the nineties was that problems caused by drug users in the public domain had to be tackled by exerting (law enforcement) pressure to undergo treatment. In every step of the judicial process, it should be asked whether treatment could be a viable option either as an alternative to detention or punishment or even during the prison sentence. Figure 1 gives an overview of the different stages of that process.

Some of these filters were specifically used to "coerce" or "funnel" drug using offenders in treatment either by early intervention or while in prison. The use of these different options or filters within the law enforcement chain has been part of an extensive project of the probation division of the Dutch Mental Health branch organisation; this project has been evaluated extensively in 1998 (Drang op maat, 1998). The main aim of the project was to use the criminal justice system as a lever.

Figure 1 gives an overview of the entire law enforcement chain from contact with the police, arrest etc. until imprisonment and post detention aftercare. Dutch prison drug policy cannot be understood without a schema of this process. It shows that at a number of points – on entry, during the adjournment phase and court session – treatment is offered as an option or a condition (ie. conditional sentence).

Within the law enforcement chain, a number of projects were implemented (the number in brackets refers to the number in table 2.):
a) Early intervention (1)
b) Drug free wings/ Prison drug support units (VBA's) (4,5)
c) Treatment as alternative for detention (5)/Inpatient Motivation Centres
d) Community order (4).
These projects were embedded in a broader perspective which aimed both at increasing the inpatient capacity to treat drug users and at the implementation of effective programmes for reintegration of the drug users. The early intervention (a) project is outside the prison domain as well as, by definition, the community order (d).

The options (b) and (c) are situated within the domain of the prison system and will be dealt with in a separate section.

6.1 "Entry" and "exit" options"

a. *Early intervention*

Early intervention projects were implemented on 26 locations in the Netherlands. The main aim of the project was to offer arrested drug users (arrested at least four times during the previous year) a choice between detention or inpatient treatment. The probation officer is the liaison officer between the client and the other parties involved. The main results were:

- a sharp rise in the number of early interventions carried out;
- an increase in occupancy rates (over the years the average time in treatment increased) and a decrease in accessibility. In 1995, 25% of the interventions resulted in program enrolment; in 1997 only 16%;
- a decrease in the dropout rate. From 54% in 1995 to 36% in 1997;
- although there was a sharp increase in the total number of early interventions, the absolute number of drug user enrolling remained relatively stable.

Figure 1: The chain of law enforcement (Source: *Drang op maat; 5 jaar aanpak justiabele drgusverslaafden;GGzNl, 1998*)

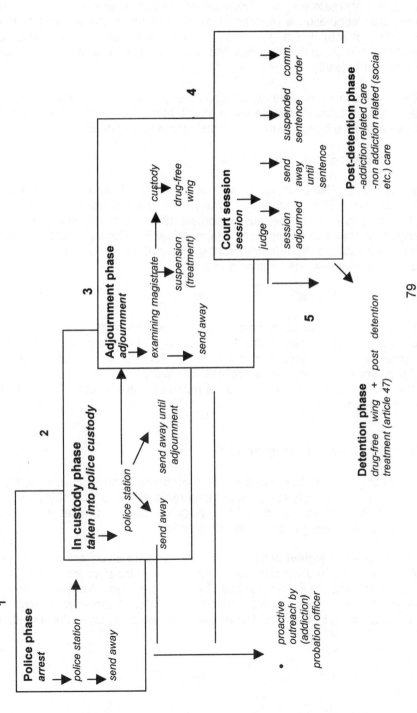

79

The effectiveness of early intervention has been evaluated on various locations. One of the main questions asked in this respect is "effectiveness" in comparison with what? (Rigter, 1999). For example, in the city of Utrecht the rate of recidivism decreased with 70% as well as the mean number of offences. Although in practice lots of users choose the treatment option, a large number drop out of treatment. It is however not known what percentage of the total drug user population is reached by early intervention, nor the long term effects in terms of reducing or stopping drug use. Although it is only circumstantial evidence, it is estimated that the rate of recidivism is as high as 90% (Tielemans, 1998).

Early intervention is an entry option, while community orders and enrolment in an Inpatient Motivational Centre are both exit options. They are offered as an alternative or a special condition in the sentencing framework.

c.   *Inpatient Motivational Centres*

Since 1996, 136 beds have been opened in 11 treatment centres in the Netherlands. The main target group was sentenced drug users causing multiple problems in the public domain and not being willing to follow the regular pathway to an inpatient treatment centre. Central in the programme is the stabilisation of the offender during a stay of three months. The programme will be evaluated at the beginning of 2000.

d.   *Community order*

For a number of years, community orders, were thought of as not being fit for drug users. A community order is issued as an alternative for an unconditional sentence of a maximum of six months. The number of community orders issued for drug using offenders has increased from 800 in 1995 to 3 200 in 1997. Due to a lack of monitoring not much can be said about the effectiveness of this modality.

7.   Dutch prison drug policy

In the beginning of the seventies, drug problems invaded Dutch society; at the beginning of the eighties the authorities realised that prison started to become part of this domain. Since then a body of rules and regulations has been growing, embodying Dutch prison drug policy.

A number of treatment options for sentenced drug users are within the domain of the prison. Two options stand out: first a number of so called alternative detention measures and second the drug free unit. These options will be described here and existed before the other interventions and projects described above. The first (treatment) units were set up in the mid-eighties; a time when it was estimated that about one third of the detainees were drug users (van Alem, 1994).

7.1 Principles

As a matter of principle, correctional settings have to be safe, humane and cost-effective. In safeguarding these principles drugs have had a marked effect on the prison environment. Currently it is estimated that 50% of the inmates in correctional institutions have problems with drugs. This means that if a crude estimate is made, from the total population in contact with the criminal justice system – in 1997 there were 40 836 detainees – approximately 20 000 are drug users.

Table 3 presents what is known about the prevalences of drug users in prison as presented in four recent studies in different prisons in the Netherlands.

Table 3: Prevalence of drug addiction in the Dutch prison system

	Koeter e.a. 1998	Van der Hurk 1998	Bieleman e.a. 1999	Schoemaker e.a. 1999
Location	Amsterdam	Rotterdam Doetinchem	Krimpen a.d lissel, Vught, Amsterdam	Scheveningen
Kind of detention	Regular detention	Regular detention/ Open Prison	Regular detention/Drug free unit	Regular detention/ Drug free unit
Sample size	330	156	89	158
Prevalence drug addiction	44.3 %	71%	74%	43%

Comparing and evaluating these prevalences can't be done without being well informed about the underlying populations and the selection taking place before entering the different types of detention centres. At the best they give low and high bound estimates of drug addiction in prison[1]. Besides different instruments were used to assess drug addiction.

In line with the Dutch drug policy, a pragmatic approach has been taken. Within prison, the quality of the detention climate has been taken as a point of departure to implement a number of measures to decrease traffic, trade and

---

[1]   Bulten (1998; page 65) found a prevalence (life time or recent) of about 50% diagnosed with the disorder drug misuser. The main object of the study was to assess mental health problems within prison).

drug use in prison and to increase the availability of treatment and warrant the continuity of care for drug users. Currently prison drug policy has 4 main tenets:

a.   Protection

Drug users who are motivated to undergo a treatment programme have to be able to do so in a protected environment.

b.   Screening/surveillance

If there are special programmes there has to be a selection procedure and follow-up before and during the programme.

c.   Discouraging drug use/import, trade and traffic

The detention climate has to be controlled (a kind of "zero tolerance zone") in such a fashion that drug use, illegal drugs imported in the institution and the presence of drugs is minimised.

d.   Basic care

As a matter of principle, basic care is provided to those who, although drug users, do not want to take part in a special programme tuned to the needs of detained drug users.

e.   Special care

Special care is provided to those motivated to undergo treatment. Currently only a small percentage of the drug users are "forced" to go into treatment.

These tenets both underlie a number of operational safety measures and are the basis of specific drug related treatment services within the prison. Safety is warranted by urine-controls, official visits, cell inspections and sanctions when using, importing or possessing hard or soft drugs.

Formally drugs are forbidden within the correctional system. In practice however, the use of soft drugs is tolerated (Zorg Achter Tralies, 1999). A small recent survey found out that of those using drugs during detention, 45% used cannabis (Bieleman, et.al., 1999). Urine controls and bodily inspection are used to detect drug use and imported or hidden drugs. If drugs are detected sanctions are taken; what sanctions are taken depends on the prisons. A national framework or national standards are lacking in this respect.

7.2 Health/addiction care in prison

Guidelines for healthcare in prison are laid down in the Penitentiary Act. They guarantee a basic level of healthcare delivery within the institution. About 28% of the registered drug users are on methadone in the Netherlands. Methadone is an established substitute drug in the Netherlands.(Ladis Kerncijfers 1998).

Although a uniform methadone policy based on common guidelines is lacking, the practice of methadone programmes within prison is threefold:

a.   a "no methadone" policy, which exists only in a minor number of detention centres. The main reason for this policy is that if detainees entering have been on a reduction programme in another detention centre;

b.   methadone reduction programme; 60% of those applying for methadone enter this type of programme which is mainly for heroin users who want to kick the habit (mean dosage: 30-40 mgs.);

c.   methadone maintenance programmes are uncommon, especially in the larger detention centres. Maintenance programmes are mainly restricted to those on a short stay, drug users with a long addiction career and drug users with severe mental health problems.

In practice, it is the general practitioner of the detention centre who is responsible for the dispension policy; this could imply a "no methadone" stand (Timmermans, 1998). From the little research that is done, it is estimated that about 4% of the detainees is on methadone (Zorg Achter Tralies, 1999).

Overdose is a rare phenomenon; death and drug overdose only occurred in a very few cases (Zorg Achter Tralies, 1999). Some say there is a relation between a period of abstinence (a period in prison) and risk of overdose after discharge. This theme - as well as needlestick incidents in prison - has not been investigated thoroughly (Timmermans, 1998).

Drug users cause a number of specific problems like behavioural problems and problems caused by detoxification or craving. Although this is a recognised phenomenon which medical doctors and prison personnel have to deal with, little is known "in fact".

8. Prison as an exit option

As was described in figure 1, prison can be used as an exit option or gateway to further treatment. In contrast to early intervention or community order, drug users are selected already undergoing a prison sentence within the criminal justice system.

8.1 Alternatives for detention measures: principles and practice

A number of regulations facilitate the practice of treatment during detention - after having served part of the sentence - outside the detention centre. They deal with drug users sentenced with a condition (see phase 4 in figure 1). There are however a number of specific conditions before an offender can be enrolled: a drug user has to be motivated to undergo treatment, the sentence may not exceed six months and over 50% of the sentence has to be served previous to the treatment programme. Discharge or drop out before the agreed date automatically means that the drug user has to return to prison. Data are available on the so-called "article 47 programme", one of the main three alternatives to detention.

From the main results of this programme over the period 1994-998, it can be concluded that the total number of appeals for the "article 47 programme" averaged about 120 individuals per annum (maximum 157, minimum 95). The programme can be completed in combination with a stay at a drug free unit. Currently about 75% of the article 47 admissions is previously enrolled in a drug free unit programme.

The main conclusions for this type of intervention were:

- an increase in the number of programme completers.
- a relative growth in referrals to rehabilitation centres.
- a better match between patient and programme.

8.2 Drug free wings

Drug free wings operate within the prison system. Alternative measures such as those described above can be used in combination with a stay on a drug free wing.

Capacity and programme

Since the late eighties, so called "drug free wings" were introduced both as a "safe haven" for drug users motivated for treatment and as a link to continuing care after discharge. Table 3 gives an overview of the current capacity within the different modes of detention.

84

Table 4: Cell capacity of drug free programmes (1998)

Remand centres	
men	298
women	13
Total	311
Prisons	
women	13
long sentences	73
short sentences	31
juveniles	48
Total	165
Total capacity (used)	476

Of the total cell-capacity, only 3.6% is used for specific drug free programmes; in about half of the detention facilities there are drug free wings. The service is run by probation workers of the outpatient drug and alcohol care. The aim of their work is to prevent relapse and to promote reintegration after discharge.

Generally, there are three phases - acting as a funnel - in which candidates are selected for a drug free wing:

1. *Screening and selection*

In this phase, information is given by probation workers about drugs, safety regulations, sanctions and options for treatment. In a small number of group sessions suitable candidates are selected. The selection is carried out by special selection officers, while the case management component is done by the probation officer.

1. *Placement and follow-up (for selected drug users)*

The programme has three elements: group work, individual care planning (post-discharge) and phase care programming so that the last part of the detention is in the region were the drug user is living. After discharge enrolment in a clinical (inpatient) programme is possible. From 1999 it is also possible to be released on "social grounds" and follow an outpatient programme.

2. *Placement and follow-up (standard procedure)*

Drug users, not willing or not yet motivated to undergo a special programme, get individual attention and counselling.

The way drug free units are operated is mainly determined by their management. In practice this means that units are operated differently (Bieleman et.al., 1999).

8.3 Practice of drug-free detention

In spite of the enormity of the drug problem in prison, drug free detention is still a niche policy. The struggle for optimal accessibility and better continuity and integration in non-law enforcement drug schemes are the main themes for these units in the late nineties (Amoureus, 1999).

- Detention centres only partly succeed in guiding drug users - via drug free units - to specific centres for alcohol and drug treatment or rehabilitation.

- If users were asked how they experienced their stay on the drug free unit, they reported that the programme was too much aimed at drug free living and psychological counselling instead of practical help for daily problems and in preparation of discharge (finance, work, housing etc.). These are however, data from a small sample (Bieleman et al, 1999).

- Occupancy rates for most centres are too low, although there is local variation. The main reason for this has been the sharp increase in cell capacity. The probability that drug using offenders were sentenced increased because of this, while at the same time the average length of stay decreased. Consequently, the eligible target group for drug free units diminished in size.

- Originally, a phase wise enrolment programme was developed before entering a drug free unit. In practice, however, this could not be implemented because of lack of trained personnel.

- Most drug free units are occupied by detainees from the own detention centre. Originally, however, it was meant for these units to be occupied by a much broader target group.

9. Prison and change

Imprisonment should be a lever for change and can be a hazard as well. Drug users deserve extra attention in this respect and Dutch policy underlines this.

Measuring change implies a baseline in time from which the amount of change over time can be measured. This could be established by a national registration or information system. The TULP registration - a national registration for offenders in custody or prison - registers the item "addiction". In practice however this item is not registered in a reliable, standardised way. In the future however this should be the case. Thus the status at the point of entry giving information on a number of relevant variables is not known. Material that will be presented here is only "snapshot evidence" from various Dutch research projects.

The underlying model to answer the five questions posed by the Pompidou group is depicted in figure 2. At the point of entry there are in fact three groups to be distinguished; *1. non users, 2. non identified drug users and 3. identified drug users.* On imprisonment, all these three groups could be involved in change either beneficial or adverse, depending on their status on arrival. From a small recent survey, it turned out that 91% of the offenders used drugs or alcohol before their sentence; for two thirds of this group their primary drug is either cocaine or heroin; other studies also point to poly drug use (Bieleman et.al., 1999; Bulten, 1998).

If a dynamic picture should be drawn, it would be possible to describe the adverse as well as beneficial changes. An adverse change for instance, could be the change from a non-drug user to a drug user, from a soft drug user to a hard drug user, or from a non-injecting user to an injecting user.

Figure 2:   Patterns and changes in drug use.

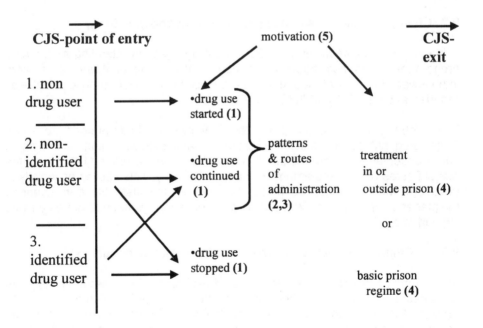

9.1. Changes in starting/continuing drug use

There is no standard procedure were every prisoner's drug status is screened by urine analysis, so a baseline status from which change could be measured is lacking.

Only one small recent survey (N=91) explicitly devoted attention to the subject of changes in use (Bieleman etal, 1999). If prisoners were asked if they used drugs during detention, 68% confirmed this statement. These groups however were not classified according to the breakdown given in figure 2. Cannabis was the most prevalent drug used (45%) besides methadone (22%), cocaine (11%), heroin (9%) and other types of drugs (9%).

In a small research project on aftercare for drug using prisoners, eighteen people were interviewed (eleven prisoners and seven ex-prisoners). The majority of ex-prisoners continued using during detention and stopped using after detention (Verwoerd et al, 1997).

Generally, soft drug use is tolerated in prison. However, the extent of the use is not known.

9.2 Changes in patterns of use (frequency, quantity, setting)

In a study of Haastrecht et al (1998), 188 drug injectors attending methadone programmes who had been imprisoned in the previous three years were interviewed. Any use of cannabis, heroin or cocaine during imprisonment was reported at 55%, 37% and 20% respectively.

Most probably, there are changes in the quantity of methadone used (not as an illegal drug but as substitute medication) in and outside prison according to some observations (Zorg Achter Tralies, 1999; Timmermans, 1998) and the actual figures of the Amsterdam Methadone Registry. This applies especially to prisoners with a longer sentence who were previously on a methadone maintenance programme. Methadone in prison is always handed out as a liquid instead of a pill.

9.3   Changes in routes of administration (risk behaviour)

For a number of years, the prevalence of registered drug users injecting has remained stable in the Netherlands, around 13% (LADIS Kerncijfers 1998). Besides it is known that certain subpopulations prefer not to inject, but inhale, or sniff or smoke their drugs. As to HIV status there are no (reliable) data; although the estimates say seropositivity is low as well as AIDS.

A recent report by the Dutch Health Inspectorate gives an estimate of 4% HIV positive; these were self report data (Man, 1998; Zorg Achter de Tralies, 1999). The last figures available about AIDS, testing and HIV status are from 1994.

Whether drug users engage in unprotected sex is not known, nor if they engage in illegal tattooing while in prison.

In a study of Haastrecht e.a. (1998) 188 drug injectors attending methadone clinics were interviewed. Five injectors (3%) admitted to having injected in prison but no sharing of needles and syringes was reported. Contrary to findings from other countries, low levels of HIV risk behaviours occur among imprisoned drug injectors in the Netherlands.

9.4 Changes in patterns of treatment (continuation, start, disruption)

Van den Hurk's study on the effectiveness of a drug free detention treatment is one the few studies giving a deeper insight into the continuity of treatment (van den Hurk, 1998). One of the main conclusions was that after one year the "drug-free detention group" (in comparison with the standard regime group) searched more actively for and accepted treatment. No differences were found for a number of outcome measures like drug use, recidivism, or physical, social and psychological problems. From Bulten's study (Bulten, 1998) on young sentenced offenders we know that those offenders diagnosed as misusing drugs, had more often had contact with outpatient addiction care. Often however they had multiple pathologies.

From the way treatment is organised in prison, implicitly an "abstinence" ideal can be discerned and consequently patterns of treatment almost have to change. However only a sketchy picture can be drawn of this.

If methadone is given, the average dose of methadone is significantly lower in prison as in other methadone-programme related centres. Drug users attending methadone clinics do not always receive the same dose of methadone in prison. Reduction of the dose is more common than maintaining. Developments like the distribution of bleach - to clean injecting equipment) have not been implemented in the Netherlands as for instance in some Australian areas (Levy, 1999).

In practice, not much is known about the taking over of responsibilities and the (free) exchange of medical information both facilitating the continuity of care. According to self reporting, 46% of the detainees stops medication on entry; for about 41% of the detainees the underlying motives for this action were not explained (Zorg Achter de tralies, 1999).

As was indicated previously, the counselling given in a drug free programme is mainly psychological and should, according to a small survey, be more practically directed to financial issues, housing etc. (Bieleman et al, 1999; Verwoerd et al 1997). So according to the opinion of detainees, the orientation of treatment should cover more dimensions.

9.5 Changes in motivation to stop drug use or to enter treatment

As was previously described there is an increasing number of people entering early intervention programmes, but the capacity of VBA-places is not fully used. From the national drugs and alcohol database (LADIS Kerncijfers 1998) we know that about 24% of those clients referred to an outpatient treatment centre are referred via a probation officer; in 1997 this was 22%.

Jongerius et.al. (1997) evaluated whether a special programme for drug users (with coercive placement) in an Amsterdam detention centre contributed to referral to treatment. About 25% of drug users were referred to regular treatment; 50% of those referred succeeded in finishing the programme. Jongerius et.al. (1997) point to the fact that motivating drug users to follow a special programme is a time consuming activity, sometimes taking longer than a month.

Dutch prison strategy towards drug users involves identifying drug problems as soon as possible and offering a programme for those who ask for treatment. Inmates who do not ask for treatment are placed in a very basic regime with work, regular urine tests and sanctions for drug use (Goutier 1997). The effectiveness of this policy on the motivation to stop drug use or to enter treatment has not been evaluated. Although community orders were increasingly applied for drug users in the last few years, nothing is known about their effectiveness in terms of changing certain pervasive patterns of drug use.

10. Conclusion

In comparing features of the Dutch system - concerning treatment as well as the way the criminal justice system operates - with other national prison systems, an unambiguous set of terms will be necessary to describe the way how "law in the books" and "law in practice" works. This report showed that:

- As to "law in practice" a number of essential key figures necessary to describe input, throughputs and outputs specifically related to drug users is lacking.

- A longitudinal view on the drug users career, as he/she passes through the criminal justice system, can 't be given; essential information on entry is (still) not registered in a valid way.

- The criminal justice system may – at it's best - for some users be a lever for beneficial change.

- Patterns of change of drug users within the Dutch correctional system can't be understood without insight into the total range of law enforcement sanctions available. They work as filters and determine the group that finally ends up in prison and the selective group who is eligible and motivated for treatment.

- Some patterns of change are induced by the fact that there is a difference in policy outside and inside the prison. The main example is methadone; there are diverging opinions in this respect. Outside prison methadone maintenance is a well grounded form of treatment; inside prison it is not.

- Although not explicitly stated, abstinence seems to be the central aim once drug users enter the prison system. Given this aim it is doubtful whether the quality of care (in terms of continuity, physical and mental help) is optimal or if this aim is realistic (Zorg Achter de Tralies, 1999).

- It is probable that the selection of those seeking treatment within the criminal justice system has improved. More drug users starting their treatment finish it according to plan. On the whole however it is not known what percentage of the (registered) drug population is reached by interventions. What we do know is that – given the relatively high estimates of drug users coming into contact with the correctional system– the cell capacity specifically meant for this group is small.

- Concerning certain adverse patterns of change, like transferring from a non drug user to a drug user, or from a non-risk to a risk category (for example in the case of injecting, needle sharing, HIV status and engaging in unprotected sex), no information is available. On the basis of the few selected studies, the prevalence of the aforementioned risk behaviours is estimated to be low.

- Although the use of soft drugs is tolerated, it is not known in what way this affects the pattern of change for the individual drug user or non drug user.

- A longitudinal (health) record of the detainee is not available in such a way that indicators of change can be assessed.

11. Discussion

In Dutch drug policy, the treatment of drug users in prison has always been an issue that has been dealt with in a pragmatic way. Within the criminal justice system links have been improved as has its first strike capability through early intervention and diversion to treatment. This under the verdict that treating drug users who commit offences, cuts crime rates more effectively than putting them in prison (Jones, 1999)

The main reason why so few aggregate data is available on the subject of change is the highly decentralised way in which detention centres and prison can collect and aggregate their own information. This was confirmed during talks with various key representatives. The lack of this makes it hard to monitor longitudinal changes within a user's career as well as transfers between various treatment and criminal justice localities. In this respect initiatives could be taken to connect the criminal justice system in a broader information strategy aiming at completing treatment demand information.

This could partly be existing initiatives in the Dutch drug policy such as the extension of the national alcohol and drugs database LADIS within the framework of the National Drugs Monitor (NDM) - as well as the European context. Since 1997 a European core item set to monitor treatment demand has been developed (EMCDDA, 1998).

Moreover, all the different parties dealing with drug users and the theme of change – probation and rehabilitation workers, medical doctors in and outside prison – have their own information repositories. These are not tuned to new themes emerging like co-ordination of care or information exchange between professionals whether they are in or outside the prison domain. There are however initiatives for an information systems strategy which makes it possible to link and verify information on detainees within the criminal justice system (Grijpink, 1997). These initiatives could facilitate efforts to improve and monitor co-ordination of care for drug users independent of where they are.

This report has mainly been based on available data and impressions from professionals. Maybe more specific and further research with the National alcohol and drugs data base (LADIS) or the Central methadone registry (in Amsterdam) could reveal more "process information" on the number of registered drug users annually arrested, remaining in custody or imprisoned. Currently the information available can be considered "snapshot evidence".

12. Summary

The aim of this report is to answer a number of questions covering the theme of patterns of change in drug use in prison. The answers to these questions are described within the context of the Dutch drug policy and the practice of Dutch law enforcement regarding drug users. In this respect two themes emerge:

- Within the criminal justice system there are a number of options to "coerce" drug users into treatment. This occurs from the moment of first entry as well as in later stages of the law enforcement process.
- Imprisonment is only one of the options available for drug using offenders, besides early intervention, community order, and other alternative measures.

The domain of this report – drug users in prison – contains a highly selective population, ie. those ending up with a prison sentence.

Information on patterns of change was collected on the basis of three sources; literature, data of registration systems and interviews with key representatives.

Estimates of the prevalence of drug users in prison range between 40-70%; About 50% is accepted as an average estimate.

Question 1: Change in starting continuing drug use

From a small number of surveys it can be concluded that both soft and hard drugs are used in prison. Evidence is lacking whether this use is a continuation of previous drug use or a start of new drug use.

Question 2: Changes in patterns of use

There is a change in dose for drug users on methadone prior to their imprisonment, specifically drug users with longer sentences.

Question 3: Changes in routes of administration

Injecting in prison exists but is very rare. Sharing of needles and syringes has not been reported so far. The prevalence of HIV within the Dutch prison system is estimated to be very low.

Question 4: Changes in patterns of treatment

Although there is a change in policy, abstinence is still the main goal within the criminal justice system. This in contrast with the "low threshold" drug policy outside the prison system. However the current policy is under review.

There is ample evidence that disruptions in the continuity of care can be prevented by taking part in a special (drug-free) programme. However there is a discrepancy between the need of detainees and the contents of the programme.

Question 5: Changes in motivation to stop drug or to enter treatment

Most drug users in prison have had prior contact with drug services. Special programmes aimed at motivating drug users to enter treatment for certain categories of drug using offenders have been implemented and will be evaluated.

In collecting information on patterns of change of drug users, the criminal justice system is a missing link. Currently only "snapshots" are available of selective populations and programmes.

13. References

Alem V. van, L.H. Erkelens, G.M. Schippers, M.H.M. Breteler en J.M. Becking (1989). Verslavingsproblematiek in penitentiaire inrichtingen. Justitiële Verkenningen, 15, 2, 39-61.

Amoureus, M. (1999). Detentie als voorbereiding op terugkeer. Overlastpost, 40-42. Uitgave van de Stuurgroep Vermindering Overlast, s.l.

Bieleman, B. and Laan, R. van der (1999). Stok Achter de deur; onderzoek naar het functioneren van de zorg voor verslaafde gedetineerden. Bureau Intraval, Groningen.

Biernacki, P. (1986). Pathways from heroin addiction: Recovery without treatment. Philadelphia, Temple University.

Bulten, B.H. (1998). Gevangen tussen straf en zorg. Psychische stoornissen bij jeugdige kortgestrafte gedetineerden. Academisch Proefschrift. Vrije Universiteit van Amsterdam.

CBS statistisch jaarboek, 1998. Centraal Bureau voor de Statistiek. Voorburg, 1999.

Continuiteit en Verandering. Ministerie van VWS, Rijswijk, 1995.

Drang op maat. Vijf jaar integrale aanpak justitiablele hard drugverslaafden (1998). GGZ Nederland, Utrecht.

Dwang en drang in de hulpverlening aan verslaafden (1988). Handelingen der Tweede Kamer der Staten Generaal, 1987-1988, 20 415, nrs. 1-2.

EMCDDA (European Monitoring Centre for Drugs and Drugs Addiction). Annual report on the state of the drugs problem in the European Union (1998). Luxembourg, 1998.

Erkelens, L.H., V.C.M. van Alem (1994). Dutch Prison drug policy: towards an intermediate connection. (In: Between Prohibition and Legalisation; the Dutch experiment in drug policy. Ed: E.Leuw and I.Haen Marshall). Kugler Publications, Amsterdam.

Facts in Figures (1999). Dutch National Agency of Correctional Institutions. Ministry of Justice, the Hague.

Goutier, J. (1997). Drug strategies in Dutch prisons. Report of the 3rd European conference on drug and HIV services in prison. February 1997, Amsterdam. Cranstoun Drug Services London.

Grijpink, J. (1997). Keteninformatisering; met toepassing op de justitiele bedrijfsketen. Staatsdrukkerij en Uitgeversbedrijf (Sdu), Den Haag.

Haastrecht, H.J., J.S. Bax and A.A. van den Hoek (1998). High rates of drug use, but low rates of HIV risk behaviours among injecting drug users during incarceration in Dutch prisons. Addiction, 9, 1417-1425.

Hurk A. van den (1998). Tussen de helpende en de harde hand. Academisch proefschrift, Katholieke Universiteit, Nijmegen.

Jones, J. (1999). Drug treatment beats prison for cutting crime and addiction rates. British Medical Journal, 319, 470.

Jongerius, J.A.H.M. and M.W.J. Koeter (1997). Drang tot verandering? Haalbaarheid en effecten van een drang- en dwnagbenadering van drugsverslaafden in detentie. Amsterdam Institute for Addiction Research, Amsterdam.

Koeter, M.W.J. and G.C. Luhrman (1998). Verslavingsproblematiek bij justitiabele drugsverslaafden. Amsterdam Institute of Addiction Research (AIAR), Amsterdam.

Ladis Kerncijfers 1997 (1998). IVV. Houten.

Ladis Kerncijfers 1998 (1999). IVV. Houten.

Levy, M.H. (1999). Australian prisons are still health risks. Medical Journal of Australia, 171,7-8.

Man, T.J.H. (1998). HIV en AIDS bij gedetineerden; het probleem en de omvang ervan in gevangenissen en huizen van bewaring. Modus, 7, 3, 8-12.

Prisons (1999). Dutch National Agency of Correctional Institutions. Ministry of Justice, the Hague.

Rigter, H. (1999). Justitiele drang en dwang bij de behandeling van verslaafden: helpt het? Overlastpost, 40-42. Uitgave van de Stuurgroep Vermindering Overlast, s.l.

Schoemaker, C. and Zessen, G. van (1997). Psychische stoornissen bij gedetineerden. Trimbos Instituut, Utrecht.

Silvis, J. (1994). Enforcing drug laws in the Netherlands. In: Between Prohibition and Legalisation; the Dutch experiment in drug policy. Ed: E.Leuw and I.Haen Marshall. Kugler Publications, Amsterdam.

Timmermans, A. (1998). Leven in de bajes. Mainline, 3, 12-15.

Tulkens, H.J.J. (1988). Graden van vrijheid; over hervormingsmogelijkheden van de vrijheidsstraf. Gouda Quint, Arnhem.

Verwoerd H. and K.Hofman (1997). Aftercare for drug using prisoners. Report of the 3rd European conference on drug and HIV services in prison. February 1997, Amsterdam. Cranstoun Drug Services London.

Veiligheidsrapportage 1997 (1998). Ministerie van Binnenlandse Zaken (BIZA). Den Haag.

Verslavingszorg Herijkt; Achtergrondstudie (1999). Raad voor de Volksgezondheid, Zoetermeer.

Zorg Achter tralies (1999). Een onderzoek naar de kwaliteitsaspecten van de gezondheidszorg in penitentiaire inrichtingen. Inspectie voor de Gezondheidszorg, Den Haag.

Key figures interviewed

F. Ambrosini (*The European Network on Drug and HIV/AIDS Services in Prison, Cranstoun Drug Services, London*)

Dr. M. Amoureus (Ministry of Justice)

Dr. F. Boom (Chairman of the platform "drug free wing" -coordinators)

Prof. dr. W. van den Brink (Professor of Psychiatry and Addiction, Academic Medical Centre/ University of Amsterdam)

Dr. E. Bulten (Psychologist, Correctional Centre Vught)

Dr. A. van der Heide (Ministry of Justice)

Dr. K. Hofman (Center for Addiction Treatment Drenthe, Assen)

Dr. A. van den Hurk (Dutch Mental Health Branch Organisation; Division probation)

Dr. J.W.M. Remmen (Health Inspectorate Utrecht and Flevoland)

Dr. C. Schoemaker (Trimbos Institute)

Dr. J. Verhagen (Ministry of Justice)

Dr. van Zonneveld (Ministry of Justice / TULP registration)

Portugal Report

Luisa Machado Rodrigues

1. Introduction

This report refers to the Portuguese contribution to the European update on *Drug Use in Prison* as a first output (Muscat, 1999) of the project *Drug Use by Prisoners* (Machado Rodrigues, 1999) developed in the framework of the Pompidou Group.

Some effort among European organisations has been made to improve knowledge in this field; the available data on drug use are not enough to get an overview of the European drug-related situation in prisons.

Among the main networks[1] interested in that important topic, two stand out in particular. One is the *European Network on HIV/AIDS and Hepatitis Prevention in Prisons,* whose objectives include harm reduction in prisons. Obviously due to the fact that drug use is one of the HIV/AIDS related problems, the analysis of drug related behaviours stands out among the targets of this network. The available report (Weiland et al., 1998) contains, among the drug variables under analysis, the following: use of illegal drugs by prisoners, routes of administration and drug treatment. *The European Network on Drug and HIV/AIDS Services in Prison (Cranstoun Drug Service)* which targets the development and evaluation of drug and HIV services in prisons. Contacts with each European Union (EU) country were made to report the situation and to estimate the proportion of prisoners who were problematic drug users (based in 1994/95). The average proportion of prisoners estimated from 189 questionnaires answered by countries (data from official, non-governmental and academic organisations) was that 46.3% were all users of illegal drugs before their imprisonment.

On the whole, because of the contradictions of the system whatever the country, it is not easy to approach the problem, since on the one hand, not only trafficking but also the consumption of opiates and other psychoactive substances are illegal. On the other hand, since both to recognise the problem and to accept to provide measures to avoid/prevent it depends on the assumption of the multiple forms of the modern drug culture, in particular those witnessed by Western society. Especially when this deals with correctional services, the complexity of the problem is more evident either from a political and technical point of view or focused on the field itself.

---

[1]   The author also thanks Ms. Weiland from Germany and Mr. Stevens from UK. They agreed to share information on the networks referred to above aiming at the co-ordination between projects.

In Portugal, especially since the late 80s, although the problem remains complex, policies are improving.

In 1993, the legislation on drug use and drug trafficking, and on the control of narcotics, psychotropic substances and precursors was revised.

As regards the drug related problems in prison, attention is mainly focused on epidemiology and treatment. In particular in the 90s new measures were provided and new projects in the field of prisons were undertaken.

2. Legislation

The decree-law n° 15/93 of 22 January revised the earlier legislation and adapted the Portuguese legislation to the provisions of the 1988 UN Convention. Either a) the illicit production and trafficking of drugs or b) the drug possession and consumption are punished. Penalties vary according to the type of crime and drug and are heavier for a) than for b). However, should the quantity of drugs seized exceed the average consumption and individual needs for a defined period (in days), the penalty may also be imprisonment. When the accused agrees to voluntary treatment, the court may suspend the sentence but this is not a widespread alternative. The goods seized from illicit drug traffic return to the State, to the Ministry of Justice in part, and to the correctional system.

Other decrees followed, including those dealing with the control of the licit market of psychoactive substances and on money laundering.

3. National survey on drug use by prisoners

In 1989, the first epidemiological survey at national level was carried out, covering a representative sample of prisoners (male and female) from all central prisons (Machado Rodrigues et al., 1994). The reported lifetime prevalence of use of illegal drugs (any) before the imprisonment among the inmates was respectively, 62.24% for men and 54.55% for women. For the same sample, but in prison, these rates were respectively 48.46% and 20.47%. These data show that the prevalence rates among the same individuals were higher before prison than in prison.

Aiming to develop a direct indicator by asking the prisoners on an anonymous and confidential basis their reported drug use, it was foreseen to conduct the survey regularly. But time ran out and only now has it been decided to conduct the study again. The second stage is planned for 1999 and will give the opportunity to obtain comparable data between a time-period of 10 years.

It is important to notice that it was in this context that Portugal proposed the project *Drug Use by Prisoners* in the framework of the Pompidou Group. Due to the interest in this type of survey, not only national initiatives but also European partner agreements were set up.

4.   Drug treatment in prison

Overall, health facilities in the correctional system targeting drug addiction include free drug units and consultations.

The central prison of Lisbon has a drug free unit modelled on a therapeutic community (Wing G with two sub-groups and forty-two beds). There is another drug free unit in the same prison which is more like a drop-in centre (Wing A with eighty-five to ninety beds) and where inmates can stay either for a maximum of one year in the programme, or move after three months into another unit. Four other central prisons have treatment units (around 100 beds) including some in the second largest city of the country (Porto). In another prison outside Lisbon, there is a drop-in centre (twelve beds) the after-care unit, which follows up treated prisoners whose penal status enables them to follow a programme targeted to work outside the prison. Again in Lisbon there is a small unit (eight beds) in another prison targeted to motivate preventive inmates to go into treatment (a programme of three months that covers the drug addicts and their families).

The philosophy of programmes vary in Portuguese prisons (psychotherapeutic, psychosocial, and maintenance programmes). In-patient facilities refer to the drug-free units and outpatient facilities are mainly by protocol with the national network for treatment of drug addiction from the Ministry of Health (CAT/SPTT), where technical teams come into the prisons or the inmates go with guards to the treatment centres. The mobility of inmates inside the penitentiary system ensures that they stay in the available units/programmes, depending on the state of their drug addiction. Co-ordination with the probation services is aimed at avoiding interrupting treatment, either when inmates enter the prison or are released.

In short, treatment programmes for drug addicts in prison are similar to those outside the prison. The psychosocial and psychotherapeutic programmes last about one year while maintenance programmes vary (both methadone maintenance and LAAM maintenance are available). In female prison wings, the available facilities care for women and their children under three years old.

It is important to notice that the prison system foresees extending the health network inside the system; a new law in the field was proposed. It is expected that this will be implemented this year. That way, health professionals will be stimulated/motivated either to move into the system or to co-operate more intensively from the outside to treat inmates.

5. General data - Update 1998

On 31 December 1998, the general situation as regards the correctional system was as follows:

Total number of prisons

There are fifty-three prisons, eighteen out of them are central, and thirty-five local. Central prisons include: (a) one psychiatric clinic targeting prisoners the court considers to be mentally ill, and (b) one prison hospital, one training prison for juveniles, and 1 women prison. The local prisons include two women's prisons. In addition to the above-mentioned prisons, there are also specific wings in other central and local prisons.

Total number of inmates

The total number of prisoners on 12.31.98 was 14,598, including the mentally ill inmates. In relation to this specific type, there were 185 on 12.15.98. Because of the mobility of prisoners, the 1998 revised data categorised by sex are still not available. The provisional data estimates the total population of women at around 11% of the prison population. According to what is expected in prisons, the male population prevails in the system. Among all prisons, the local ones represent about 7% of the total population in the correctional system.

Total number of non-citizens

There were 1,560 (10.69%) non-citizens among the total number of prisoners. From these, 1398 (9.58%) were male and 162 (1.11%) were female. Their distribution by region and sex is included in table 1.

Whatever the sex, non-resident prisoners were mainly Africans. In relation to other nationalities, there were more European men (18.17%) than men from Latin America (9.94%). On the contrary, there were more women from Latin America (34.57%) than from European countries (19.75%). However, the proportion of inmates from these countries was higher for women than for men. From these data, the hypothesis is that these cases are more traffic-related than consumption-related, needing further analysis to be confirmed or refused. Among the former Portuguese African countries, Capo Verde was highlighted. In fact, 31.40% of men and 25.30% of women were inmates from this country. It is important to notice that the largest immigration movement in Portugal is from Capo Verde.

Table 1: Distribution of non-citizens, by region and sex

Region	Male		Female		Total	
	number	%	number	%	Number	%
Africa	960	68.67	69	42.59	1 029	65.96
Angola	229	16.38	11	6.79	240	15.38
Capo Verde	439	31.40	41	25.30	480	30.77
Guinea	102	7.30	3	1.85	105	6.73
Mozambique	43	3.08	1	0.62	44	2.82
Sao Tome	38	2.72	7	4.32	45	2.88
Other	109	7.80	6	3.70	115	7.37
Latin America	139	9.94	56	34.57	195	12.50
Europe	254	18.17	32	19.75	286	18.33
Other	45	3.22	5	3.09	50	3.21
Total	1 398	100.00	162	100.00	1 560	100.00

(*Source: DGSP*)

Total number of convicted inmates

The total number of inmates convicted was 10 348, representing about 70% of all prisoners from the date referred to above.

Total number of inmates awaiting sentence

At the same time, there were 4 250 pre-trial detentions (29.11%).

Total number of inmates by sex aged over 18

Ages categorised by sex are not available. The distribution by age group among the total of prisoners is described in the following table:

Table 2: Distribution of inmates over 18, by age

Age group	n	%
19 – 24	2 531	17.34
25 – 39	8 696	59.57
40 – 59	2 793	19.15
≥ 60	335	2.29
Total	14 355	98.34

(*Source: DGSP*)

Data available show the more frequent class of age range from 25 to 39 years old, including 59.57% of inmates. The median age was 29.5 years old. There was a certain similarity between the quantity of inmates aged 19-24 (17.34%) and aged 40-59 (19.15%). However, due to the fact that the available age classes show various intervals, it is impossible to get a clearer idea on the distribution of ages.

Juvenile inmates by sex aged 18 or under

243 inmates were aged between 16 and 18 years old, but only 1.66% of the prisoners was under age. Data by sex are not available.

Highest completed education level of all inmates

According to the data available on levels of educational among prisoners, described in the following table, inmates mainly reached the primary school (67.50%). This figure is in accordance with what is known in this field.

Table 3: Distribution of inmates, by educational level

Educational level	n	%
No school including no reading and no writing	1 045	7.16
No school but reading and writing	1 058	7.25
Primary school	9 853	67.50
Secondary school	2 426	16.62
Tertiary education	113	0.77
Other	103	0.71
Total	**14 598**	**100.00**

(Source: DGSP)

It is interesting to note that from about 1% of the prisoners who reached university level and about 16% of those who reached secondary school, a sub-group similar to the figures for workers of Eurasian ethnic origin may be found. These indicators point to the special needs as regards schooling, training and work targeting of that category of inmates who may be a minority but who appear as a significant part of the population in the prison system.

6. Discussion

Whatever the problems and difficulties are when dealing with drug addiction, its complexity starts in the concept itself. The main question (Agra et al., 1993) continues to be: is this crime, illness or both?

The simplest answer would be both; however, discussions on decriminalisation of certain drugs show we are facing a construct society which may modify according to the evolution of modern ideas, especially, those which concern the relationship between drugs and the legal, penal, judicial and judiciary systems.

The social tolerance to drug-related crimes by reducing penalties when consumption is associated with them or providing treatment as an alternative to prison show the health dimension is increasingly taking the place of the criminal one. Therefore, the point is to ensure that society is protected from drug-related crimes like robbery, theft, murder, and other insoluble ones.

The contradiction is more evident when we are faced with, in opposition to that tolerance, the public hostility as regards drug addicts, the homeless, and especially their sexual habits. Should this be interpreted or not as a kind of "last resort" healthy behaviour to legally obtain drugs before moving into the next stage of their drug career, such as criminality? To get the message across, to revise policies, and to provide measures that include the prevention of the drug problem as a whole and in prison clearly appear as a priority.

In spite of the networks and the drug/crime surveys available in Europe, the lack of wider and comparable information in this domain is evident (Turnbull & Webster, 1997). There is also an urgent need for policy-makers and professionals.

From what is known in the field, it is expected that prisons will house more and more drug-related inmates with a majority of men, and where the rates of women, non-residents, and drug-related crimes will increase (Facy, 1997). It is also expected that the drug problem is more and more widespread among the general population (Ramsay & Percey, 1996) where socio-economic factors and the use of prohibited drugs vary according to age, and where the current use appears as a predictor of drug addiction within its crime-related problems.

Moreover, it is no surprise that drug-related offenders may be well-educated, women are frequently involved in drugs trafficking and in prostitution (Chaiken & Johnson, 1988); inmates, in general, are a risk population (Strang, 1993) as regards non-protected sexual behaviour and injecting behaviours.

The assumptions that drug addiction and trafficking are major public health and security problems (Setbon, 1995), and that the repressive models to combat/prevent the drugs problem (Brochu and Frigon, 1989) are incomplete and fail, point to changes, where other policies should take place. It is expected that these will be supported not only by a variety of facilities (Walmsley & Joutsen, 1998) but also by a deep knowledge of the problem in so far as this will be better described using appropriate means.

A growing number of recommendations (Kriznik, 1998) are targeted more and more frequently at the clarification of the situation in prisons as a mean to contribute to new policies and facilities. Portuguese priorities as regards drug addiction in prison go along with this line and the Pompidou Group project, mainly centred on the impact of prison in the treatment of drug addiction (Pompidou Group, 1999), serves as a part of these needs not only at a national but also at a European level.

7. References

Agra, C., Teixeira, J. M., and Fernandes, L. (1993). *Dizer as Drogas. Ouvir as Drogas.* Porto: Radicário

Brochu, S. and Frigon, S. (1989). Toxicomanie et délinquence: une question d'éthique, *Revue Internationale de Criminologie et de Police Technique*, Genève, 2, Avril-Juin, 163-171

Chaiken, M. R. and Johnson, B. D. (1988). Characteristics of different types of drug-involved offenders, *Issues and Practices in Criminal Justice,* Washington D. C., National Institute of Justice

Facy, F. (1997). *Toxicomanes incarcerés,* Paris: Editions Médicales et Scientifiques

Kriznic, I. (1998). 12th Conference of Directors of Prison Administration – Conclusions, *Penological Information Bulletin*, Strasbourg: Council of Europe, 78-80

Machado Rodrigues, L. (1999). *Drug Use by Prisoners –Revised Project Proposal,* Strasbourg: Pompidou Group, P-PG/Epid (98) 16 rev E

Machado Rodrigues, L., Antunes, C. Mendes, Z. (1994). *Prison Surveys – Portugal,* Report to the "Seminar Management of Drug Addicts", Athens, 3-5 March 1994, Lisbon, GPCCD

Muscat, R. (1999). *Drug Use by Prisoners –Guidelines,* Strasbourg: Pompidou Group, P-PG/Epid (99) 12 E

Pompidou Group (1999). *Drug Use by Prisoners – 2nd. Working Meeting – Summary of the discussions,* Strasbourg, Pompidou Group, P-PG/Epid (99) 14 E

Ramsay, M. and Percy, (1996). *Drug misuse declared: results of the 1994 British Crime Survey*, London, Home Office

Setbon, M. (1995). Drogue, facteur de délinquence? D'une image à son usage, *Revue Française de Science Politique*, Paris, vol. 45, 5 , 747-772

Strang, J. (1993). Sexual and injecting behaviours in prisons: from disciplinary problem to public health conundrum, *Criminal Behaviour and Mental Health*. Whurr Publishers Ltd., 3, 393-402

Turnbull, P. J. and Webster, R. (1997). *Demand reduction activities in the criminal justice system in the European Union – Final Report*, Lisbon, EMCDDA/CRDHB

Walmsley, R. and Joutsen, M. (1998). Prison populations in Europe and North America: problems and solutions, *Penological Information Bulletin*, Strasbourg, Council of Europe, 81-86

Russian Federation Report
Criminality and drug abuse in places of confinement

Research Institute on Addictions, Russian Ministry of Health

The topics of both the prevalence of drug use and the relevant criminality were for a long time taboo for the press, which created the impression that there was no problem. This was accompanied by the distortion of statistical reports of law-protecting bodies and the practical realisation of the concept of the alleged steadfast lowering of the crime level as socialism progressed (Karpov V. G., Lissovskaya E.V., 1988).

Nevertheless, until 1924, penal responsibility came into effect for production and possession, with the intent to sell, and for the sale of psychoactive (stupefying) substances. The perfection of the criminal legislation in this field was leading to the hardening of responsibility for drug-related crimes. In 1926, the penalty for the production, possession and sale of psychoactive substances was a prison sentence of one to three years; in 1986, it was ten years. Numerous investigations and statistical data indicate that the number of convictions for drug-related crimes in 1966-1975 had doubled, in the following period up to 1982 the increase doubled again; by 1993, the rate had doubled again (Yakubovich A.E.,1988).

In 1986, when society's attention focused on the problem, the registration of illegal activities involving drugs had increased sharply by 49.1% and the registration of activities carried out with the purpose of selling, had increased to 135.7% in one year (Bogolyubova T.A., 1998).

It is obvious that in the 70s and 80s, drug abuse was becoming increasingly widespread. Young people were being drawn into this vicious circle with ever increasing rapidity.

Drug use has often assumed an organised form (dens, common use companies). At the beginning of 1986, the attention of the press to the problem did bring it into the "open" and the close connection of the prevalence of drug use with criminality began to be statistically confirmed.

The juridical literature reveals that half of the drug abusers, as a rule, had committed a crime. Among such persons, the rate of those who had been previously convicted is high. The covering up of the problem into the 80s limited the volume of investigations in this field; nevertheless, it is clear that when drugs are not in free circulation, the acquisition of drugs as such is part of the crime. It does exclude the cases when, for an example, an adolescent is "treated by his friends". The second line of criminality supposes action, aiming at finding the means of acquiring drugs, resulting in drug users committing the so-called "mercenary crimes" (Tyazhkova I., Zubkova V., 1990).

It is stressed in the juridical literature, that the features of drug-related criminality (duration, multi-components, relapse character, traits of organised criminality, latency), sustain and ensure the steady broadening of "reproduction" of illegal drug use for non-medical aims.

In the last year, the steady growth of various kinds of drug-related registered crimes has been noted. Therefore, the volume of this kind of crime, during the 1991-1998 period, has increased ten times. For example, in 1991-1997, the number of trafficking crimes had increased thirteen times and both persuasion to use drugs and organisation and upkeep of dens for drug use four times. Parallel with the growth in the number of registered crimes in the field of illegal drug trafficking, there was the growth in the number of persons who had also committed a crime. In 1991-1997, this figure increased in Russia 6.5 times; the increase was more than five-fold for the number of women, almost four-fold for the number of minors, six-fold for the number of persons who had no steady income and six-fold for those who had already committed crimes. It is important to note that among unmasked criminals of this kind, the proportion of Russian citizens was 92.6% in 1992, 92.1% in 1994, and 94.8% in 1996.

T.A. Bogolyubova, basing himself on the results of the statistical data analysis of the past ten years, came to the following conclusions (1996):

- Criminality connected with illegal drug trafficking increases. "The criminal medium" is so satiated with these processes that the registration of criminality in this field is being accomplished effortlessly by low-protection bodies. Nevertheless, the information on the scope of prevalence of illegal drug trafficking is approximate. The majority of those kind of crimes remain latent.

- The indicated tendency was formed a long time ago and it remains stable. The immediate consequence of this process is the intensification of drug use prevalence among the population.

- Drug trafficking in Russia is carried out mainly by Russian citizens.

In the juridical literature, the problems relative to peculiarities of criminality in the field of illegal drug trafficking are widely elucidated. However, the investigations, which highlight the problems of drug use by persons kept in places of confinement, have appeared only in the last decade.

The realising, by the society, of the big scope of the problem of drug use prevalence, of the connection of this phenomenon with criminality, of fatal consequences of these processes in the future and, as well, the growing "openness" of the problem had resulted in the broadening of investigations in this field.

The example of such an investigation is the concrete sociological work, fulfilled in the 70s by A.A. Gabiani (1990). This investigation, being the first and the only at that time, gives the legal, social and psychological characteristic of the "narcotism". Though the work is based on the materials, collected in the Georgian Soviet Socialist Republic (SSR), its theses and conclusions are, up to this time, of scientific and practical significance on the background of the complication of the problem in the Russian Federation. The work is done in two stages: 1967-1974 and in the year of ten years later.

In the territory of the Georgian SSR, a total of 1 200 persons were questioned, including 500 persons in places of confinement.

The majority of drug abusers in places of confinement are men (91.7%). However, the rate of women among the prisoners had increased almost five times during the ten year period. The proportion of persons under 20 years old has almost doubled.

In the 1980s, 66% of all respondents were convicted for the illegal production, acquisition, possession, transportation, carriage or trafficking of psychoactive and other drastic toxic substances.

It is worth mentioning that, in the 70s and 80s, it was mainly drug users rather than drug traffickers who were kept in the places of confinement.

The author asserts that drug use is closely connected with urbanisation: 87.1% of the respondents live in towns. During ten years, the rate of persons living in medium-sized and small towns has increased considerably.

During the period of investigations, the rate of persons who had previous convictions had increased (28.1% and 47.1% correspondingly). The differences in educational levels of imprisoned drug users, as well as of their parents, had disappeared. The welfare standards of the convicted respondents had increased: if in the 1970s 46.2% of them lived in families where the income was below average, in the 1980s the rate of such persons was only 16.4%. There were a noticeably large number of respondents in the places of confinement without a family or divorced ones. The majority had no children.

More than 14% of the respondents lived in families where family members used psychoactive substances or alcohol (13%).

The questioned drug users talk readily about the state of their health, but their awareness of the fact that health is undermined and that recovery in the conditions of confinement is impossible, create such a state of mind, that medical treatment is considered by these persons as having no prospects.

Changes have taken place in the popularity of used psychoactive substances. In the 1960s and '70s morphine was the most popular drug (68%). In the 1980s, it was hashish (83.9%). The rate of persons who systematically use the drugs in places of confinement is very high. It was revealed that 84% of the inquired persons use the drugs two times a day and even more often.

In the course of the investigations, it was discovered that from 78.8% to 96.6% of drug users cannot abstain from drug taking, but more than 60% of all the inquired persons regard their weakness critically.

According to the duration of the consumption of psychoactive substances, the rate of persons who use drugs during one year of staying in places of confinement is 5%. The rate of those who use them for ten years and more is 28.6%.

The author revealed one more important circumstance. In the 1970s the number of those who used drugs regularly in places of confinement was 17.9%. In the 1980s the rate had increased to 57.6%.

In such a way, as the earlier work of A.A.Gabiani has already shown distinctly, the abuse of psychoactive substances is widely spread in places of confinement. On the one hand, this is connected with the general unfavourable dynamics of the phenomenon among the population, on the other hand, the high concentration of drug users in correctional institutions favours the spreading of drug use there.

The information about the number of drug users in places of confinement is discrepant, as the data given by various investigators indicate. The compulsory court ordered medical treatment serves as the indirect indicator of this.

As the census of the convicted persons indicates, 0.8% of the total number of those serving their sentences in correctional/labour institutions (C.L.I.s) are those who are ordered to undergo compulsory medical treatment for drug abuse (0.7% of general regime convicted persons, 0.4% of hardened regime convicted persons and 1% of special regime convicted persons. From these figures in each of these regimes, the percentage of women is 0.4% (Bogolyubova T.A., Tolpekin K.A., 1991).

The author underlines the imprisonment as such is not the factor which ensures overcoming dependence on a drug (more than 96% of drug abusers say that they cannot get rid of the drug craving). In other words, in a C.L.I. such persons have the potential to be law-breakers to committing repeated crimes.

According to various data, in some years, up to 50% of all crimes in places of confinement were committed concerning the consumption of a psychoactive substance or alcohol. It is worth mentioning one more detail: nearly 70% of the convicted persons link the origin of the drug craving with the staying in places of confinement (Bogolyubova T.A., Tolpekin K.A., 1991).

Mikhlin A.C., Novikov A.A., Voloshin N.I. (1979-1991) give, using the data of the census of convicted persons in 1979, the following data about the court ordering of compulsory treatment for drug abuse. In general regime correctional/labour colonies the compulsory treatment for drug abuse was ordered to 0.7% of convicted persons; in hardened regime colonies the indicator was 0.4%; in hard regime ones it was 1.1%; in special regime ones it was 1%. In censuses of convicted persons carried out before 1979, namely the censuses of 1926, 1970 and 1979, such data were not registered and thus they were not analysed. In colonies with all kinds of regimes, the compulsory treatment for drug abuse was ordered to 1.2% of imprisoned women.

Later works, based on the results of analysis of materials in criminal files, contain somewhat different quantitative characteristics. Therefore, Miroshnichenko N.A. (1984) gives the data, which indicate that compulsory treatment for drug abuse was ordered to 2.4% of the convicted persons. According to the data of Smetenko V.N. (1989), the treatment for drug abuse was implemented to a third of all persons convicted for drug-related crimes. In 12.3% of the cases the treatment was prescribed by a psychiatrist only. In 7.6% it was prescribed by a psychiatrist and a psychotherapist. In 80% of cases it was prescribed by a psychiatrist, a psychotherapist and a neuropathist; the prescription was made by the expert commission only in singular cases (this research was carried out with the use of very voluminous material: more than 1 600 criminal files and 8 000 of other court materials were consulted).

According to the data of Brilliantov A. A. and Oligov V. I. (1993), the compulsory treatment for drug abuse was implemented in 89.4% cases of the total number of convicted drug abusers.

The official statistical data show that in 1990-1992 there were 4.8 thousand people ordered into compulsory treatment (0.9% of the total number of convicted persons were compelled to treatment for drug abuse) (Grishko A.Ya., 1993). The same author had questioned 1 400 of those imprisoned in C.L.I.s and more than 600 drug abusers in medico-labour and medico-educational institutions. It was found that 66.3% of those ordered into compulsory treatment were minors. In this category of persons the willingness to be treated lowers with age: 83% of 16 year-olds are willing to be treated compared to only 3% in the group of those aged over 18. The author mentions that among drug abusers who committed a crime, 90% do not think they are ill.

The rates indicated by Aliyev V. M. (1990), are close to those mentioned above: more than 80% of the questioned drug abusers who committed a crime, continue to abuse drugs. According to the data of Galiulina Sh.N. and Ponomarev S.N. (1988), nearly 25% of drug users had starting using drugs when staying in places of confinement. In 1992 Alargaladze A.Ya., trying to give the number of drug abusers in C.L.I.s, had indicated the following rates: 28.7% of the total number of convicted persons have the diagnosis "drug abuse"; in 0.8% of these cases, the diagnosis was established in the C.L.I.

Edelman A.I. (1992) reaches a more general conclusion: the absolute majority of all the convicted persons who serve their sentence in places of confinement were using drugs before their conviction (or were participating in illegal drug-related activities). The author gives several concrete examples. In the town of Irkutsk half of those detained for such crimes as pick-pocketing and stealing from homes were drug users. The criminal groups which were committing particularly dangerous multi-episode crimes in the town, were in twenty-seven cases (of a total of thirty-one) consisting mainly of drug users. From such categories of persons who are registered in internal-affairs bodies and are called "racketeers", "thieves-in-law" and "thieves' authorities" only certain individuals have not consumed drugs. But it is precisely these individuals who are the background organisers of drug trafficking and ensure the widening circle of drug users.

It is possible to indicate some additional quantitative characteristics: 77.5% of registered law-breakers in the field of illegal drug trafficking are drug users. Among those who were convicted for other crimes, 10% had started using drugs in L.C.I.s (Pakhomov V.D., 1996; Firsakov S.V, 1996). Annually nearly 0.2% of all crimes were convicted in a state of drug intoxication ("Dynamics of criminality in Russia", 1994).

Parallel with the sharpening of the problem a large number of research projects dedicated to the studying of socio-demographic characteristics and the personality features of convicted drug abusers are being carried out.

The age pattern of convicted drug users (according to statistical data) is relatively stable: 38% of those aged 18-24; 26% of those aged 30 and over; 25% of those aged 25-29 and 11% of those aged 16-17.

The age fluctuations within this contingent of persons in the period 1989-1992 was 1-2%. The rate of women has increased to 5.9%. The rate of school children and students was 7%. 47% of these were from professional training schools, 31% were high school and professional secondary school students ("Dynamics of criminology in Russia", 1994; ed. Dolgova A.I.).

Aliyev V.M. (1990) carried out the study of socio-demographic characteristics and the social type of personality of convicted drug abusers (400 convicted persons were included in the survey) from the point of view of understanding the subjective causes of the behaviour which leads to crime commitment. It was shown that 67.5% of all the convicted persons are men aged 18-30. 63.1% had secondary school educational level; 83.7% are physical workers and 52% were unemployed for one year before the crime was committed.

More than half (50.4%) of the surveyed persons began using drugs under the age of sixteen. The main kinds of drugs used are opiates 43.9%; mixed substances (poly-drug using) 33.8%; hashish 15.9%; barbiturates 4.5% and stimulants 0.6%. The author points out that the progress of poly-drug use is characteristic at stages which precede crime commitment. The commitment of crimes was in 89.2% of cases related to drugs. 29.3% of crimes were committed with the aim of acquiring drugs and 7.8% of crimes were committed in the state of abstinence. More than 70% of crimes committed by drug users were not directly related to drug trafficking.

For drug users, as well, the relapse into criminality is usual: 26% of them are convicted at least twice; 3.8% of them are convicted five times or more.

As far as psychic anomalies are concerned, the surveyed persons presented alcoholism (22.3% of cases), psychiatric disorders (14%) and organic illnesses of the central nervous system. It was found that 78.9% of the surveyed persons had personalities with a well-defined anti-social orientation. The author revealed three types of personality among those drug abusers who had committed crimes.

1. Persons characterised by introversion and autism. The main reason for starting to use drugs is the desire "to join a group of people" and "to overcome the feeling of alienation".

2. Persons with leadership skills.

3. Persons for whom the main reason for using drugs is the impossibility of adequately satisfying their needs.

One of the author's main conclusions is that those drug abusers who had committed a crime continue to use drugs after the conviction (81.5%) (Aliyev V.I.,1990).

The results of the social investigation of Galiulina Sh. N., Ponomarev S.N. (1988), carried out in five C.L.I.s in various regions of the USSR are close to the material described by Aliyev. As to the age, 63% of convicted drug users were less than 24. At the time of arrest 67.8% of the persons surveyed were unmarried. Before the conviction 37% were unemployed. Some of those employed had considered their work as low-paid (30%), monotonous (29%), dirty (19%), hard (18%), with no prospects (7%) or not to their taste (18.8%). The overwhelming majority of convicted drug abusers (79%) had committed a crime related to the production, possession or trafficking of drugs. A third of all the drug abusers had begun using drugs regularly in places of confinement. The most popular drugs are hashish, opium and mixed substances (poly-drug abusers). Those who did not intend to stop drug use totalled 30%.

The drug abusers in C.L.I.s are inclined to form groups on the basis of "being countrymen" (59%) or "common interests" (22%).

Thus the majority of investigated persons had committed crimes related to drugs. As a rule, a long period of drug abusing preceded the crime. Convicted drug abusers in C.L.I.s are those who break the rules more often, are worse at

111

adapting to forced labour and regarding educational, correctional and treatment actions, than other prisoners. The main features of the personality of a drug abuser (individualism, unscrupulousness, dishonesty, opportunism, the desire "to go with the flow" and "to live in the present") promote the formation of motives for committing a crime. The steadily growing asociality of the person provokes relapses of criminality.

Alargaladze A.Ya (1992) carried out an epidemiological analysis of clinical-social characteristics of convicted persons suffering from drug-related disorders and serving their sentences in C.L.I.s. The majority of those surveyed were 18-25 years old (85.57%); 63.5% did not have definite occupations and 90% did not have a family. The majority had completed secondary education (57.7%). The diagnosis "drug abuse" involved 28.7% of the convicted persons. A first time diagnosis of "drug abuse" was made in C.L.I.s in 0.8% of cases. In the analysis, the psychopathological features of the character and various psychopathological disorders were noticed in 87.2% of cases. Most often the dependence on opiates, barbiturates and hashish was found.

Alferov Yu., Sereda E.V., Kozyula G.G. (1989), using psychological techniques, had singled out four kinds of drug abusers in places of confinement, according to the extent of personality degradation.

1. Drug abusers without personality degradation (up to 15%) with a positive attitude towards the demands of the regime (especially when they are sure of an early discharge) who agree to undergo medical treatment.

2. Drug abusers with a primary degree of personality degradation (up to 20%) with an adequate attitude towards their situation who also agree to undergo medical treatment.

3. Drug abusers with partial personality degradation (up to 45%), who disrupt the regime, evade labour and decline treatment.

4. Persons with an inadequate attitude towards situations and towards themselves, who do not work, remain completely indifferent to educational actions and decline treatment (up to 20% of those questioned).

Among the convicted drug abusers psychopathological disorders are observed (55-65%). In 22% of cases, the pathological features are caused by illness. Nearly 80% of drug abusers require structured medical observation.

The authors conclude that the personality changes alone of drug abusers define their behaviour in a colony.

Firsakov S.V. (1996) indicates the following socio-demographic data on convicted drug abusers. The rate of minors convicted for illegal drug trafficking was 7.9 % and it rises from year to year. The rate of women was 9.5%. The rates of other convicted persons are as follows: manual workers 24.6%; office employees 2.6%; those occupied in commercial structures 7.9%; intellectuals 1.8 %; agricultural workers 1.8 %; students 0.9 % and entrepreneurs 0.9 %. 59.5% were employed yet with the minimum level of education. Such an occupation pattern remains characteristic for convicted drug abusers over a period of several years, but the rate of those without an occupation is increasing. For example, during 1993 it had risen to 27 %. A further example is that of 111 persons detained in Moscow in August 1994, only four were occupied.

Among surveyed persons, 21.6% began to use drugs under the age of 14; 27.5% aged 15-17; 14% aged 18-30 and 3.9% over 30. 63.8% first used drugs in company and 13.8% when alone.

More often than not the convicted persons were drawn into drug use by adults who had previous convictions (in 30.7% of cases).

The author concludes:

• the most "criminal" contingent includes the persons who began to use drugs in the earliest years;

• among the persons who were convicted for drug-related crimes, only 10% have not been through secondary education, which confirms the connection of early drug abuse with the rapid degradation and lowering of social status;

• the use of drugs is the determining feature of the personality which influences the possibility of committing crimes.

Drug craving is, as a rule, the main cause of crime. Smetenko V.N. (1989) in such a way depicts the "portrait" of the drug abuser, convicted for activities connected with illegal drug trafficking: a man approximately 24 years old; previously convicted; a drug user, known, as a rule, to internal affairs bodies and to the health services. At the time of offending he is in a state of drug intoxication (stupefaction). The author points out that more than 64% of the surveyed convicted persons in this category were previously registered in medical institutions; 47% of persons use mainly opiate derivatives; 12% use cannabis products originating from cannabis and 3.4% are poly-drug abusers. The author mentions, like other investigations (Alargaladze A.Ya., Alferov Yu.A. et al., Aliyev V.M. et al), that the analysis of the majority of surveyed persons indicated various psychological disorders.

Drug dependence is the main cause, leading to crime to get money to buy drugs.

Special attention should be paid to the personalities of convicted drug-using women (Boychak A., 1996), because drug abuse quickly brings a woman to social degradation: in 80% of cases the women lose their family; in 92% of cases they become unemployed. The data of this investigation show, that the personality of 83% of convicted drug-abusing women, even before their regular use of drugs, was characterised by the following peculiarities: the psychological complex of sharing in asocial behavior; the yearning for new, unexpected impressions, the origin of which is, for this category of women, drug use. Only 10% were occasional users. The common personality features of convicted drug-abusing women are: 70% of them consider their behaviour as normal. They do not feel guilt towards their relatives. 58% of them are not able to assess neither their past, nor the future. The majority of them (63%) do not have any concrete life goals, except drug use. Two thirds of marriages are concluded with drug-abusing men.

On the whole, the personality characteristic is as such: hedonistic orientation, egoism, a low level of control of the emotions and behaviour at all; a lack of moral and value barriers and an inclination towards parasitism and sponging.

The drug-abusing women commit theirs crimes mainly with a view to obtaining drugs.

Pozdnuyakova M.E. (1995) carried out, using a somewhat different approach, the investigation with the purpose of studying the personality characteristics of a drug-abusing person and his social needs and links. Men with the diagnosis "drug abuse" in hospitals and in hardened regime C.L.I.s examined. Several cardinal human needs were selected for study: achievement; recognition; the acquisition of knowledge; the removal of stress; security; a rising standard of living and leadership.

The investigation showed, for example, that the surveyed person had a low need of achievement. Their need for recognition and communication was combined with an early use of drugs and alcohol. The need for a rising standard of living and for prestige is distorted among drug abusers into the aspiration for achieving esteem in their own circle. The need of leadership was high among the majority of participants in the survey, but it took the form of authoritarian behaviour and the desire to bend the surrounding people to their will at any price. The author concludes that drug abuse replaces and distorts many of the personality's needs and is used by human beings to try to correct a discordant personality on the whole and its motivational pattern, which can favour the commitment of crimes. One more aspect of the problem under study is the pattern of committed crimes and the relapse into drug-related criminality.

Khruppa I.S. (1984) has examined 360 criminal files concerning drug-related crimes. He has shown that the most frequent crimes are misappropriations: "secret withdrawals" (54% of crimes), that is thefts of raw materials such as parts of poppy plants or cannabis plants etc. to make drugs; 32% of crimes are "official frauds"; 4.6% of crimes are "open thefts"; 2.3% of crimes are misappropriations connected with violence. The aim of all crimes which are committed is to obtain drugs.

Tyazhkova I. and Zubkova V. (1990) give the data concerning the character of drug-related crimes committed by fifty drug abusing adolescents. They are: profiteering (57%), misappropriations (21%), crimes against personal property (32%) and offences against the person (13%).

Pakhomova V.D. (1996) reports that among the convicted persons serving their sentences in C.L.I.s as drug abusers, 59.6% had committed drug-related crimes and 40% of them are convicted for mercenary crimes as well; 44% of them are persons with the last conviction for drug-related deeds and, more, with previous convictions for other crimes. Only 2% of convicted drug abusers commit violent crimes later.

The pattern of drug-related criminality: trafficking (12.2%); possession (62.2%); production (46.9%); stocking of raw materials (20.4%); transportation and carriage (15.3%) and the organisation, management and planning of illegal operations concerning drugs (6.1%). 62.9% of these crimes are committed alone; 35.2% by members of a group of adults and 1.9% by members of a mixed group.

The activity of persons who are convicted for illegal drug trafficking is based on the steady need to get drugs (eventually, more often than not, by illegal means) because the subjects of drug-related crimes are both drug users and drug traffickers (the majority of participants in illegal drug trafficking are themselves drug users). This allows drug-related crimes to be classified as heinous or especially heinous crimes, according to theories and classifications in the criminology.

Both recidivism and organised crime of drug abusers have a special place in the pattern of drug-related criminality.

The number of drug-related crimes committed by organised groups had increased thirty-fold from 1989 to 1998. The volume of withdrawals of psychoactive substances from organised groups (in kilograms of psychoactive substances) had increased 200-fold in the same period (data of this kind are being systematically collected in Russia only from 1986, Luneyev V.V., 1997).

The unwillingness to recognise this phenomenon in this country for a long time (Brilliantov A.V., Oligov V.I., 1998) had lead to the problem being studied only in the last five years.

The authors give the following data: 34.4% of all the registered drug abusers had been committing crimes previously. Ten percent of them are minors. The publication contains the characteristics of a relapsed drug abuser, from criminalistic and socio-demographic point of view. The relapsed drug abusers make the youngest group. In the last 10 years the group of relapsed drug abusers at the age under 30 has increased from 56.7% to 98.9%. These persons have low educational level, 25% of them have no, even, the secondary education; they often descend from one-parent families; 80% of them have no a family at all, almost nobody has children.

Almost all (99.9%) participants in the survey were subjected to compulsory medical measures. Almost half (47%) of these persons were unemployed and uneducated. 45.4% of them worked on a low professional level and nearly 10% of them had neither work nor domicile. It was noted that 7.5% of drug abusers after the serving their sentences had committed new crimes in the first year of freedom and that 16% of convicted drug abusers had committed new crimes while serving their sentences. The level of group criminality is high among drug using offenders, but according to the authors' data group criminality is 30.6% of the general contingent of those convicted. As far as the pattern of crimes is concerned, illegal operations with psychoactive substances total 45.5% .

The most popular substances at the given stage of the investigations are: cannabis (79.6%), opiates (18.3%).

As the author assures, not more than 11% of convicted drug abusers are "on the way to correction". The authors conclude, that there is an acute need to study the personalities of drug abusing offenders and of a specific social post-penitentiary controlling of the behaviour of those drug abusers who committed crimes.

It is opportune to consider the problem from the view point of Shmarov I.B. and Komarnitsky S.I. (1993), who inform us that from the places of confinement in the former USSR more than 500 000 persons were being discharged annually between 1981 and 1990. They point out that the structural analysis of the data on various groups of discharged persons does not in fact exist, because in the year of 1993 there was no corresponding statistical information characteristic to this contingent, on both the socio-demographic indicators and the state of health. Such information exists only institutions which execute punishments, but even there it is not always accurate. So, in particular, the results of some research studies indicate that nearly 30% of all convicted persons confined in C.L.I.s have mental health problems. However, this information does not reach the health service directly although this contingent needs appropriate medical treatment.

In places of confinement it is the possible to use drugs. A certain part of the total number of convicted persons are accustomed to using drugs in places of confinement, as many investigations indicate.

The above allows us to conclude that registered criminality in the field of drug trafficking is increasing, as well as the number of persons who commit drug-related crimes. But, as all investigators point out, the statistical indicators which reflect these phenomenon, depend on changes in legislation and in politics, as far as the prevention of illegal drug trafficking is concerned.

Thus in connection with this, the main task is the perfection of the legislative base for the struggle with illegal drug trafficking. The second of the most important tasks is the creation of possibilities for understanding the measures of effective medical and social aid to those who use drugs after their discharge from the places of confinement.

References

Alargaladze A.Ya., Clinico-social characteristics of convicted persons suffering from drug abuse. Collected article "Problems of controlling the drugs and prevention of drug abusers" Ed. Babayan E.A.

Aliyev B.M., Personality of convicted drug abusers, individual educational influence upon them in correctional/labor institutions,. Moscow, 1960, p.22.

Alferov Yu., Sereda E.V., Kozyula G.G., Drug abusers in C.L.I.S. Personality and behaviour. "Personality of criminals and individual influence upon them" (Collection of scientific articles of Research Institute of Ministry of Internal Affairs of USSR), Moscow,1989, pp 46-54.

Bogolyubova T.A., State of narcotism in Russian Federation. Collected articles "Actual problems of deviant behaviour (struggle against social diseases)", Moscow, 1995, pp 37-48.

Bogolyubova T.A., Criminality connected with illegal drug trafficking in "Hard violence criminality in Russia at the beginning of 90s". Moscow, 1996, pp-54-62.

Bogolyubova T.A., Tolpekin K.A. Participation of interrogator and of public procurator in the struggle against toxicomania of convicted persons in Methodical text-book, Research Institute on problems of strengthening the law and order. Moscow, 1991, pp 40.

Boychak A., Drug abuse among women. Collection of articles "Problems of drug abuse prevention in modern society". MNEPU, Moscow, 1996, pp 22-26.

Brilliantov A.V., Oligov V.I., Relapse and personality of relapsing drug abuser. Socio-criminological problems in: "Relapse criminality, legal and social problems". Moscow, 1993, pp 30-41.

Voloshin N.I. et al. Description of convicted persons serving their sentences in prisons in "Description of persons, convicted to confinement". Issue 5, Moscow, 1982.

Voloshin N.I., Ivanova A.T., Kirillova I.A., Mikhlin A.K., Novikov A.A., General description of convicted persons in "Description of persons convicted to confinement". Issue 1, Moscow, 1982., p 186

Gabiani A.A., Yesterday's and today's narcotism. Tbilisi, 1988, p 256.

Gabiani A.A., On the verge of disaster., Moscow 1990, p 221.

Galiulin Sh.N., Ponomarev S.N. Implementation of confinement relative to drug abusers. Ministry of Internal Affairs of USSR. High school, Ryazan, 1988.

Gassanov E., Drug abusers are progressing in "Socialisticheskaya zakonnost" No.3, 1991, pp 34-45.

Grishko A.Ya., Legal and criminologic problems of social rehabilitation of chronic alcoholism and drug abusers. Abstracts of thesis for doctor's degree. Moscow, 1993, p 38.

Kazakova V.A., Methods of definition of level of latency of crimes in the field of illegal drug trafficking.in "Security and health of a nation in relevance to criminality". Criminological association, Moscow, 1996, pp 66-69.

Karpov V.G., Lissovskaya E.B., Ideological functionality of inadequate ideas about social diseases. Collection of articles "For the healthy made of life" (struggle against social diseases), part 1, Moscow-Brest, 1988, pp 12-13.

Kirillova I.A., Lissyagin O.B., Description of women serving sentences. In "Description of persons, convicted to confinement". Issue 3, Moscow, 1982.

Martsinkevich N.N., Prevention of narcotism as a mode of prevention of criminality. Collection of articles "Problems of drug abuser prevention in modern society". MNEPU, Moscow, 1996, pp 14-22.

Miroshnichenko N.A., Criminal responsibility for illegal making, keeping, acquiring, transportation, carriage or selling of psychoactive substances. Kharkov, 1984. p.15.

Mikhlin A.S., Novikov A.A., Description of men serving their sentences in C.L.I.S, Issue 2, Moscow, 1982, p 84.

Mikhlin A.S., Fetisov V.Z., Men serving their sentences in C.L.I.S. in "Description of persons, convicted to confinement". Issue 2, Moscow, 1982.

Mikhlin A.S., Personality of persons convicted to confinement and problems of their correction and re-education, Moscow, 1974. P31.

Luneyev V.V., 20th century criminality. World criminologic analysis., Moscow, 1997, p 500.

Pakhomov V.D., Criminalistic-legal description of the personality of criminals who abuse drugs.in "Security and health of a nation in relevance to criminality". Criminological association, Moscow, 1996, pp 59- 66.

Pozduyakova M.E., Dissatisfaction of social needs as an important factor of drug use. Collected articles "Actual problems of deviant behavior (struggle against social diseases)", Moscow, 1995, pp 25-36.

Ed. Dolgova A.I., Argunov Yu. N., Orlov A.S, Drug-related crimes in "Criminality changes in Russia (criminologic commentary to criminality statistics)". Moscow, Criminologic association, 1994, pp 208-220.

Smetenko V.N., Criminalistic-legal protection of health in USSR, Moscow, 1989. p 33.

Tyazhkova I., Zubkova V., Influence of hard drinking and of drug use on criminality among minors., Sovetskaya justitsiya., Moscow, 1990, No. 4, p 18-20.

Fetisov V.Z. et al., Description of convicted persons, serving their sentences in "Description of persons convicted to confinement", Issue 4, Moscow, 1982.

Firsakov S.V., Socio-demographic characteristics of the personality of criminals who abuse drugs in "Security and health of a nation in relevance to criminality". Criminological association, Moscow, 1996, pp 51- 59.

Khruppa N.S., Criminalistic-legal struggle against misappropriation of psychoactive substances, Kiev, 1984. p.37.

Shmarov I.V., Komarnitsky S.I., Social aspects of relapse criminality prevention in "Relapse criminality, legal and social problems", Moscow, 1993, pp 3-15.

Edelman A.I., Drug abuse and criminality. Today's tendencies and regional features in "Problems of struggle against group and organised criminality", Irkutsk, 1992, pp 28-30

Yakubovich A.E., Criminal responsibility and drug abuse in "Collection of articles "For the healthy mode of life (struggle against social diseases)", part II, Moscow-Brest, 1988, pp 21-22.

Slovak Report
Drug issues in prison establishments of the Slovak Republic

Col. MUDr. Werner Scholz

In prison establishments in Slovakia, drug addiction existed and exists in the form of the use of various substances such as antiasthmatics, analgesics, antiepileptics, volatile substances and the like. We can say with certainty that there were no hard or soft drugs or their users at all in the past in our prison establishments.

The drug scene changed after 1989. In 1993, we registered the first eight imprisoned persons who stated that they had used drugs before admission to custody. Data has been obtained on the development of drug use from 1994 to 1998, from medical searches on entry into custody or prison. A person who stated using drugs is interviewed and a "Drug addiction report" (see Figure 1 below) is written down. It is registered and processed by the Department of Health and Social Care of the General Directorate of the Corps of Prison and Court Guard of the Slovak Republic. It follows from the results obtained that opiates are the most frequently used drugs and that the most frequent route of administration is by injection. The highest number of cases is in the Custodial Institution in Bratislava.

The drug addicts are examined by the general practitioner of the institution who also organises the examination by the psychiatrist and makes a decision concerning further medical treatment. Based on the objective findings of withdrawal symptoms, fourteen persons in 1997 and fifteen in 1998 were treated in the Hospital for Prisoners in Trenčín.

To decrease the risk of infiltration of drugs into prison establishments, and also for improving the detection of drug addicts, the mobile laboratories for drug testing were managed for all institutions. These laboratories are for testing solid, liquid and powder substances and tablets and the institutions are equipped with the testing strip for quick screening of the drug in urine. The Corps own sniffer dogs for drug searching.

A protective alcoholic and drug treatment course is followed while serving a sentence of deprivation of liberty in accordance with a Law on serving a sentence of deprivation of liberty, based on a court decision. In 1998 there were two departments for voluntary drug and alcoholic treatment. The total capacity of both establishments is 41 beds.

To solve the drug problems in prison establishments a sum of 2 713 000 SKK was made available by the Committee of Ministers on Drug Problems and Drug Control, Foundation against Drugs and from the State Foundation of Health.

The solution to drug issues in the Slovak prison service is a long-term task which is worked out for individual sections of the prison and court guard. Detailed information could be provided by the director of the department for health and social care of the General Directorate of the corps.

Figure 1:Drug addiction report

Health department of the institution............................		
Name, Surname **Date of birth / Birth certificate no.**		**Citizenship** 1 Slovak 2 Czech 3 Other
Marital status 1 unmarried 2 married 3 divorced 4 widowed	**Education** 1 elementary not finished 2 elementary finished 3 secondary without graduation 4 secondary with graduation 5 bachelor 6 university	**Economic activity** 1 employed 2 student 3 unemployed 4 self-employed 5 pensioner
Drug taking **Type of accommodation**	**Route of administration** 1 smoke 2 sniff 3 eat, drink 4 injection 5 other	**Frequency of drug taking** 1 less than once in two weeks 2 once a week or less 3 from 2 to 6 days a week 4 daily 5 more than once a day
Age when first started using drugs 1 up to 15 years 2 up to 17 years 3 between 17-18 years 4 after 18 years	**Length of periodical drug-taking** 1 one month 2 less than 3 months 3 more than 3 months 4 one year 5 more than one year	**HIV tested** 1 yes 2 no
Previous treatment 1 not treated yet 2 treated once 3 treated more than twice 4 treated more than five times	**Form of treatment in this hospital** 1 dose reduction, detoxification 2 long-term substitution, maintenance 3 long-term psychosocial treatment, medication 4 advisory, supporting 5 associated	
Last treatment 1 where 2 when	**Diagnosis**	
Date, stamp, signature		

Spanish Report
Drug addiction in prison –
patterns of change in Spain

Elena Garzon Otamendi/Graciela Silvosa

1. Description of the Spanish Penitentiary System

1.1 Legal Framework

The legal framework for the actions below is defined by the Spanish Constitution, whereby prison sentences and security measures must aim at education and social integration, as well as to assure the right to health care. This constitutional disposition has been developed as a norm by means of the Ley Orgánica General Penitenciaria (Penitentiary Organic Act). This is the legal framework to assure the right of drug addicted convicts to benefit from prevention, health care and social integration programmes.

The Penitentiary Rules include actions that may be linked to the therapeutic process, such as probation, programmed leaves for specific treatment, regular transfers of convicts into the Second grade (segundo grado) to another prison, personal leaves, the serving of sentences in extrapenitentiary centres and the bringing forward of freedom on bail.

The informative brochure (5/95 IP) about "Global policy for drug-related issues in Instituciones Penitenciarias (Penitentiary Administration)" includes the execution strategies for programmes aiming at drug addicted convicts, comprising damage reduction programmes, prevention programmes, detoxification programmes and social integration programmes.

Additionally, the Criminal Code includes security measures for drug addicted individuals clear of criminal responsibility. The Criminal Code comprises the application of security measures for drug addicted individuals clear of criminal responsibility to enable treatment in detoxification centres. It also considers suspension of sentence for drug addicted individuals in some particular cases.

1.2 Organisational Structure

A close collaboration is established between the Government Delegation for the Plan Nacional sobre Drogas, the Dirección General de Instituciones Penitenciarias (General Office for Penitentiary Administration), Planes Autonómicos y Municipales sobre Drogas (Autonomous and Local Plan against Drugs), National and Autonomous Plans against AIDS, the Consejerías de Salud in the Autonomous Communities (Autonomous Health Councils) and NGOs, (these are subsidised to collaborate with the National, Autonomous and

Local Plans against Drug Abuse and with the Ministry of Employment and Social Affairs).

It is important to highlight the participation of extrapenitentiary experts by means of mixed teams for intervention in penitentiary centres. These teams, together with internal personnel, form the operative frame for intervention for drug addicted convicts. Therefore, professionals from different associations and NGOs intervene in 61.9% of centres and are members of the Grupo de Atención al Drogodependiente (Drug Dependant Care Group).

This type of organisational structure enhances the ties between prisons and the community, to assure the continuity of treatment of either drug consumers entering prison or convicts leaving prison.

2. Method

Analysed data is taken from different surveys used by the penitentiary and juridical indicator of the Observatorio Español sobre Drogas (Spanish Observatory of Drugs).

- Instituciones Penitenciarias (Penitentiary Administration) database: Statistics on penitentiary population, survey on the social and health condition of individuals entering prison for the first time (SURI).

- The treatment indicator approved by Instituciones Penitenciarias (Penitentiary Administration) in the Observatorio Español sobre Drogas (Spanish Observatory of Drugs): Instituciones Penitenciarias registered 1,755 treatments approved in 1998 reported to the treatment indicator in the Observatorio Español sobre Drogas (Spanish Observatory of Drugs).

- Annual report of the Autonomous Plans against Drugs: An annual description of users according to the type of therapy.

3. Epidemiological data on penitentiary population

3.1 Sociodemographic characteristics

The penitentiary population on 1 January 1999 amounted to 38 365 convicts, excluding Catalonian prisons, the administration of which has been transferred to the Autonomous Government. 90.8% of this population were male, 17% were foreigners, and 61% were between 26-40 years of age (4.3% were younger than 21 years of age). 73% were serving a sentence, 55% of whom were recurrent offenders. 46.4% had been convicted for crimes against property, and 32.4% for crimes against public health[1]. However, this percentage grows significantly if we consider the penal situation and whether

---

[1]   This is a literal translation of the Spanish expression, which generally refers to "drug traffic".

offenders are male or female. i.e. 78.8% of the convict population has been convicted for crimes against property and public health, which are typically drug-related crimes.

An increase of 4.73% on 1997's figure for the number of convicts in the country has been confirmed. After three years of a downward trend in figures (1995-1997), they rose again to 1996's level in terms of average population and 1995's level in terms of end-of-the-year population. We must also highlight an increase in the number of individuals aged under 21, although the average age of the convict population is gradually increasing.

In the last few years, the convict population has changed significantly. This has mainly represented an increase in the percentage of the female population, which was 5.37% of the total in 1987, while it was more than 9% in 1998. The female population has practically trebled in the last decade.

3.2 Health Profile

HIV, hepatitis C and hepatitis B are the most important among viral infections in penitentiary environments. This is due to their high recurrence and clinical consequences. The most important risk group regarding these infections are intravenous (IV) drug consumers (IDUs).

In the same way, tuberculosis also has a higher infection rate in IDUs due to their particular lifestyles as well as to an association between this disease and HIV infection. Research carried out in Spain has found a close link between the period of time in prison and the development of tuberculosis, where the two most relevant risk situations are drug consumption and imprisonment periods.

The percentage of HIV infected individuals in the prison population on 29 January 1998 was 18.3%, which may be an underestimated percentage, since some of the centres which failed to complete this variable show a high percentage of HIV infection. The percentage in HIV infected inmates in July 1997 was 20%.

On the other hand, the number of individuals receiving antiretroviral treatment on 29 January 1998 was 2 471, which represents 6.6% of the total penitentiary population at that time. This is the highest percentage recorded since the beginning of this half-yearly survey (1991) and confirms a growing trend in the use of antiretroviral treatment.

A total number of 9 933 tuberculosis cases have been registered by the Proyecto Multicéntrico de Investigación en Tuberculosis (PMIT, Multicentre Tuberculosis Research Project), a research study between the Instituto de Salud Carlos III (Carlos III Health Centre) and thirteen Autonomous Communities, from May 1996 until April 1997. The global rate for tuberculosis-HIV patients has been 6.8 per 100 000. Four percent of tuberculosis cases were convicts in prison, while 18.3% of HIV seropositive were imprisoned convicts.

A growing trend in HIV infection has been observed in the female population. Furthermore, female individuals follow more risk-conduct patterns.

3.3 Drug consumption in prisons

Around 80 000 individuals entered prison in 1986. Approximately 70% were regular consumers of illegal drugs (56 000 people). Roughly 12 000 individuals were addicted to heroin, and only 660 individuals had received some form of hospital care. In 1989, 44.5% declared that they had consumed drugs intravenously, and the average consuming period was 5 years. 28% of convicts were HIV seropositive, and in the case of drugs consumed parenterally, the number of HIV infected individuals went up to 60%.

Over 50% of individuals who entered prison in 1998 were estimated to suffer from problems related to the consumption of psychoactive substances. This percentage changed depending on the penitentiary centre.

3.4 Consumption patterns

The treatment indicator approved by Instituciones Penitenciarias in the Observatorio Español sobre Drogas (Spanish Observatory for Drugs) shows the same general characteristics as treatment approved cases entering these centres. In 1998, 1 755 individuals were registered for approved treatment in Instituciones Penitenciarias, which were reported to the treatment indicator in the Observatorio Español sobre Drogas (Spanish Observatory for Drugs). (We must take into account that reporting coverage has been low. This coverage includes penitentiary centres in Andalusia, Catalonia, Castille-Leon, Madrid and Murcia since 1996).

As in previous years, heroine is still the main cause for most approved treatments against psychoactive substances (88.9%), although cocaine is starting to represent an important proportion of cases (6%). Among cases approved for treatment for the first time, the percentage of cocaine addictions is higher (8.5%) and the percentage of heroine cases is lower.

Individuals receiving treatment for one drug, normally consume more than one type of drug apart from the main one. The most frequent secondary drugs are cannabis (58.5%), cocaine (50.5%), hypnotics and sedatives (35.4%).

With regards to the serologic condition of individuals with HIV approved for treatment, we must first indicate that the percentage of cases approved for treatment with an unknown condition is high (33.7%), although rather less than the individuals approved for treatment in the Community (43.7%). Therefore, results must be assessed with caution.

126

3.5 Route of drug administration

The treatment indicator approved by the Observatorio Español sobre Drogas (Spanish Observatory of Drugs) and the Penitentiary Administration's Unified Data Collection System points out a tendency to use the respiratory route (smoked or inhaled). An important change in the main route of heroin administration has been registered.

Important changes have taken place in the last few years, since the percentage of individual using parenteral administration of drugs has dropped to 50%, while at the same time there has been a parallel increment in the percentage of smoked drug.

On the other hand, several research studies on parenteral consumers of drugs entering prison indicate that a high percentage of this type of users has shared syringes at some particular point.

In relation to these risk behaviours, research studies suggest an increase in the risk of infection with intravenous administration of drugs within prisons compared to that of free individuals. Fewer drugs are administered intravenously in prisons, but there is a higher risk of disease infection since there is a higher proportion of individuals sharing syringes. In most prisons inmates cannot buy or exchange syringes. A lower number of individuals use this route of administration probably due to scarcity of syringes, fear of punishment or fear of infection. But those individuals who decide to use this method are running a higher risk of infection.

4. Treatment

Intervention programmes have increased in number and variety in the last decade. Programmes for harm reduction have been especially noteworthy, since they have allowed us to increase the number of convicts receiving treatment and improve the rate of treatment continuity.

Regarding intervention methods within penitentiary environments, we must highlight the following:

Syringe-exchange programmes.

There are syringe-exchange programmes running currently in three penitentiaries (Basauri, 1997; Pamplona, 1998; and Tenerife, 1999). Another three programmes will soon be set up in three other centres.

Let us say that unlike in other international programmes where dispensing machines are being used, supply and exchange of syringes is carried out by members of the staff.

Let us highlight the positive results obtained from the programme implemented in Basauri. In fact, the Ministry of Interior Affairs has recommended the development of these programmes throughout the penitentiary environment.

Methadone programmes.

All penitentiary centres have access to this therapeutical method. The number of users has grown significantly in the last few years (1996-1998). In fact, the number of opiate consumers in some of the Autonomous Communities, which have received treatment in penitentiary environments, is higher than the number of consumers in the Community aid system.

Development of drug-free modules.

Two innovative projects have been started recently: two intrapenitentiary therapeutical populations have been implemented; in one of them female and male convicts live together, and in the other one, individuals receive methadone treatment.

Diversion of drug-dependant convicts to community resources.

By means of the application of the Reglamento Penitenciario (Penitentiary Rules) drug addicted convicts can gain access to community resources. These diversions have increased in the last few years. This increment has been significant in the case of diversion to treatment at doctor's surgeries, and is related to the significant number of individuals undergoing methadone treatment.

Let us point out, to sum up, that during 1998, there has been a quantitative and qualitative increment in all programmes. If we compare this to previous years, it is to highlight an increment in the number of individuals receiving methadone treatment and in the number of individuals diverted to community resources. In the former case, the number of convicts who received methadone treatment during 1998 was 10 577, while in 1997, the number of users was 6 606. The number of convicts diverted to community resources during 1998 was 2 647, while in 1997, only 1 974 convicts were diverted.

A total number of 24 201 convicts received treatment in 1998 under a programme for the reduction of damage and detoxification.

5. Conclusions

The general penitentiary population seems to have grown, and particularly the female population. Still, the majority of convicts are male (80%), and the population has tended to be older. Around 50% of the penitentiary population suffers from drug addiction problems; the most commonly consumed drug is heroine, although cocaine consumption is growing. An increment of smoked drug compared to injected drug has also been registered. However, risk behaviours are still significant. HIV prevalence for this population is estimated around 18%.

The most common criminal profile for imprisonment falls into crimes against private property; with a difference between male or female offenders, where the most common cause for imprisonment is crime against public health. The majority of the penitentiary population is serving sentence, and over 50% of this is crime recurrent.

There is an important percentage of judicial patients in the health system as a consequence of security measures being applied. It has also been registered that most alternative serving of sentences are related to drug addiction issues.

Generally, the profile of a "judicial patient" is as follows: 30-year old male, recurrent offender, drug-related crime, poor education, poor professional qualifications, drug dependency and health problems. The description of the structure of this population and its social-sanitary situation corresponds to a population characterised by marginal lifestyle and a low continuity of all types of treatment.

Women are generally young, inexperienced offenders, from an ethnic minority in a significant percentage, single mothers with several children, poor academic and professional qualifications and with drug dependency problems. A high percentage is serving sentences for crimes against public health.

6. Debate

Most judicial patients show dependency on opiates, particularly heroin, although they are also addicted to other drugs such as cannabis and cocaine. A higher percentage of these individuals also consume drugs parenterally and suffer from a higher percentage of HIV infection.

These individuals represent a significant percentage of patients in the care system for drug addicts. Most of them receive methadone treatment. This is logical if we consider that this system was established to counter heroin-related problems and the soundly documented relation between heroin consumption and criminal conduct.

However, it has been confirmed that judicial patients commit mostly non-violent crimes and acquisition crimes. And that, generally, drug abuse leads to non-drug related crimes as well as crimes against private property.

On the other hand, a high level of crime recurrence and an increase of those imprisoned has been observed for this population. Crime recurrence and the increase of individuals imprisoned seem to be determined by drug abuse. In fact, a connection between failures in alternative serving of sentence and drug addicted individuals has been confirmed. Furthermore, several research studies lead to the conclusion that the illegal use of drugs is the main contribution to overcrowding and high crime recurrence.

There seems to be a relation between crime recurrence and robbery, as well as between crime recurrence and heroine addiction. Although research studies confirm a connection between delinquency and drug abuse, there is no general simple relation between high rate of drug abuse and a high crime rate.

In view of this, any contact with the Justice Administration is a vital opportunity, otherwise it is difficult to gain access to these individuals. They can, in this way, receive medical aid and general risks can be reduced during their imprisonment.

These findings and estimates must be taken into account when it comes to planning and designing intervention strategies. In fact, an underestimate in the number of drug consumers and related sanitary-criminal issues could lead us to undervalue fund requirements for health care of the judicial population.

Our penitentiary administration has responded by increasing and diversifying treatment services. Specifically, it has placed special importance on programmes for the reduction of damage, (although with a time delay): the development of methadone treatments into all penitentiary centres and the establishment of syringe-exchange programmes. However, if patients continue to show problems with a variety of substances such as cocaine, doctors and pharmacists will have to increase their efforts to offer a valid solution.

It is also a priority to improve the co-ordination between the Penitentiary Administration and Social and Health Services. In fact, illnesses such as HIV/AIDS, TBC and hepatitis C, as well as drug addictions require a closer collaboration between several administrations and programmes. This implies a greater application of programmes for public health in the penitentiary environment, which also requires the collaboration and co-ordination of the community public systems. (health, social and drug detoxification services).

7.   References

Chaves F, Dronda F, Cave MD, et al. A longitudinal study of transmission of tuberculosis in a large prison population. Am J Respir Crit Care Med, 1997; 155, pp 719-25.

Miranda MJ, Barberet R, Canteras A, Romero E.: Análisis de la eficacia y adecuación de la política penitenciaria a las necesidades y demandas de las mujeres presas.Instituto de la Mujer, 1999.

Moreno Jiménez, MP. Situación de internamiento versus situación de libertad: diferencias de algunas variables en presos drogodependientes. Rev. Adicciones, 1999; Vol.11(1):23-31

Morentín B, Gostín A. Análisis de la delincuencia habitual en una muestra de 578 detenidos. Actualidad Penal, 1998, 8, pp163-73.

Observatorio Español sobre Drogas. Informe nı 2. Madrid: Ministerio del Interior: Delegación del Gobierno para el Plan Nacional sobre Drogas, 1999.

Otero B, Medrano M, Gómez JL, Pereiro C, López Abajo B, Bermejo A. Estudio Epidemiológico de los detenidos puestos a disposición judicial en Pontevedra. Libro de Actas de XXII Jornadas de Socidroalcohol, 1995. p .575-81.

Pallás Alvarez JR, Fariñas Alvarez C, Prieto Salcedo D, Delagado Rodríguez M. Factores de riesgo asociados a ser usuario de drogas intravenosas en la población penitenciaria. Rev. Esp. Sanid Penit, 1999; 1: 80-87.

Ríos Martín JC, Cabrera Cabrera PJ. Mil voces presas. Universidad Pontificia de Camillas, Madrid, 1998.

England and Wales Report
The effect of prison on drug use. The situation in England and Wales

Paul Turnbull

This paper sets out the current situation in England and Wales regarding drug use in prisons. It is based on a collection of materials including published and unpublished literature and prison service data. It is divided into five main sections considering the effect prison has on: the incidence of drug use by prisoners, patterns of use, route of administration, treatment, motivation to stop use. Some summary and concluding points are made in the final section.

Background

Population based information about drug use in prison has only become available relatively recently in England and Wales. The introduction of Mandatory Drug Testing (MDT) has provided a more detailed assessment of the numbers using drugs in prison and patterns of use. However, for information about the effect of prison on drug use we have to patch together data from a range of sources. This includes prison service data and the findings of independent research studies. Most of these data were collected during the past ten years. The focus of many of the research studies was the risk of transmission of HIV among prisoners injecting drugs.

During 1998, 132 100 prisoners were held in 132 prisons in England and Wales. The average prison population at any one time was 65 298. The majority of prisoners are male (96% 62 914) and 21 years old and over (67% 43 672). At any one time 33% of the prison population is under 21 years old. Nearly half of adult male prisoners in 1998 were serving sentences of four years and above (20 760).

Incidence

Information on the incidence of drug use among prisoners in England and Wales is scarce. MDT data provides an insight into the prevalence of use of populations of prisoners but tell us little about changes in use. In order to assess changes in use we need information on the numbers of prisoners using drugs before entering prison. Such data are scarce. However, we may be able to draw some conclusions based on the information available.

Drug use prior to imprisonment

A recent study conducted in police stations with 839 arrestees found high levels of drug use (Bennett et al. 1998). Urinalysis results on 622 respondents showed that the average rate of positive tests was 61%. The most commonly identified drugs used were cannabis (46% tested positive), opiates (18%), benzodiazepines (12%), amphetamines (11%), cocaine (10%), and methadone (8%). Females were more likely to test positive for opiates. Older arrestees were more likely than younger arrestees (aged 16 to 20) to test positive for opiates and about one-third tested positive for cocaine. While arrestees are not prisoners they are likely to be prisoners in the future. Obviously this was only a small-scale study but it is now being extended and will aim to recruit 5 000 arrestees per year. In the future these data may be able to provide a proxy indicator of the drug use among prison populations.

The most extensive study of the English prison population and drug dependency prior to imprisonment was conducted in 1988 (Maden et al 1990 a,b). High levels of drug dependency in the six months prior to imprisonment were reported (by 11% of men and 23% of women). In the same time-period, 7% of men and 15% of women reported having taken drugs by injection. On the basis of these data, it has been estimated that 7.5% of the prison population in England and Wales will have injected within six months prior to imprisonment. This amounts to approximately 3 400 prisoners at any one time and 15 000 prisoners in a year (Turnbull et al, 1992; ACMD, 1993). These data are limited since they only provide information on dependency on drugs rather than the use of drugs.

In 1997 a survey of eight prisons in England and Wales holding nearly 5 000 inmates was undertaken. The overall participation rate in this self-completion anonymous survey was 83% (3 942 of 4 778). Since this study focused on HIV and Hepatitis B, information was only collected on injecting drug use and not drug use by other routes of administration. The proportion of adult male inmates who had ever injected drugs, outside of prison, was 24% (660 of 2 798). Of these, 59% (387) were "current" injectors, having injected in the four weeks prior to entering prison. The proportion of female prisoners reported having injected drugs outside prison was (117 of 410). A greater proportion, 74% (87) were currently injecting on entry into prison. Among young offenders there were fewer IDUs, only 4.2% (30 of 714) reported having injected drugs. The proportion of those who were current injectors was 42% (11 of 26).

Strangs study of HIV/AIDS risk in a sample of about 1 000 adult male prisoners found that the male prison population has experience of much higher levels of drug use and injecting behaviour than the general population. Two fifths (41%) had injected drugs in the 12 months before imprisonment.

More women prisoners have been shown to have a history of drug use prior to imprisonment. The Chief Inspector of Prisons' Survey in 1996 found that 40% of female prisoners had used at least one drug and over a quarter used been poly-drug users prior to imprisonment.

The above evidence indicates that many of those who are in prison or at risk of being imprisoned have previous experience of drug use. Between 25% and

70% were using drugs before imprisonment. While many were using cannabis, a significant minority used a range of other drugs. Many (between 40% and 60%) injected their drugs.

Drug use in prison

MDT has been operating in all prison establishments since April 1996. Approximately 10% of each prison's population are chosen randomly each month and tested for a range of drugs. During 1996/7, 24.4% of those tested proved positive for at least one drug. This dropped to an average of 20.8% for 1997/8. The highest proportion of positive tests was for cannabis (19.9% in 96/97 and 16.5 % in 97/98) followed by opiates (5.4% in 96/97 and 4.2% in 97/98) then benzodiazepines (1.4% in 96/97 and 1.3% in 97/98). The indications are for the year 1998/99 that there has been a further drop in the number of prisoners testing positive for drugs to 18.3%. Again, the highest proportion of positive tests were for cannabis (14%) followed by opiates (4.4%) and benzodiazepines (1.3%). While the rate of positive tests for cannabis have consistently fallen, rates for positive tests for opiates have tended to be fairly steady at around 4%. The Home Office speculate that this pattern may in part relate to the fact that cannabis traces remain for longer in the body compared to opiates so that the deterrent effect of random MDT could be greater for cannabis than for opiates.

In a research study looking at the effect of MDT on drug use, Edgar and O'Donnell interviewed 148 prisoners. Almost all said they had used cannabis outside of prison; half had used heroin, amphetamines, cocaine, LSD or prescribed drugs. Three out of four reported that at some time while in prison they had smoked cannabis. Four out of ten had used heroin or prescribed drugs. They found that of 111 prisoner who used drugs prior to imprisonment 30 (27%) stopped using drugs when in prison. Imprisonment and the threat of detection via MDT appear to have had a greater effect on those who use cannabis. Nearly half (46%) of those who used cannabis only in custody reported stopping using the drug, whereas only 13% of those using heroin had stopped. They also compared self-reported drug use with actual test result. They found that on the basis of self-reported data that 31% of current drug users evaded detection (17 out of 54 interviewees). The type of drug used seemed to have an effect on the chances of a current drug user going undetected. Cannabis was not found in 35% of those who said they had used it and opiates were not detected in 48% of those who reported use.

Strang's study of HIV/AIDS risk behaviour found over 600 interviewees (62%) reported using cannabis while in prison. A further 18% reported using injectable drugs in prison. Prior to imprisonment 41% reported injecting drugs.

Qualitative considerations of drug use in prison have found similar trends. Turnbull and colleagues found of a sample of 452 over half (55%) reported that they had used a drug when last in prison. The majority reported that they used cannabis, however, heroin use was reported by one in five (Turnbull PJ, Dolan

K A and Stimson GV 1991). A wide variety of other drugs were also used. Further qualitative work with 44 recently released prisoners found all respondents used drugs when they were last in prison. The most commonly used drug was cannabis followed by heroin (36) (Turnbull et al 1994). All had used drugs prior to imprisonment.

It is difficult to assess the extent to which these data show starting or resuming drug use. There are few sources of information about neophyte use in prison. Information currently available in the England and Wales relates to new use of particular drugs (mainly heroin) or new use of drugs by injection (both covered in the patterns of use and routes of administration sections). One small-scale study reported that over a quarter (27% n=30) of the sample drug users reported that they first tried heroin in prison (Edgar and O'Donnell, 1998).

Patterns of use

In this section, changes in the frequency of use and quantity used, and the types of drug used are considered. Again a range of sources of information is used.

Does the frequency and quantity of drugs used change?

There are little data on frequency of drug use in prison. However, the picture that emerges is one of a range of drugs that are regularly available, but where individual levels of drug use decrease. For example, cannabis use may compensate for decreased opiate use. Turnbull presents the following quote which illustrates a typical pattern of use for a short-term prisoner. Prior to imprisonment this prisoner used heroin on a daily basis as well as a range of other drugs.

> "I reckon I scored gear (heroin) about four or five times…when I was in there…and I scored hash about… probably the same number of times…I got…pills and stuff…Valium, Temazepam…I got a couple of Rohypnols at one stage…" (27 year old male, imprisoned for six months).

Turnbull and colleagues have also produced a detailed analysis of patterns of heroin use in prison among a small sample of recently released prisoners. Only a small number (four) had a good regular source of supply of heroin and managed to maintain their heroin use without interruption while in prison. Most reported that they carried on using opiates after withdrawal when they first came into prison, but attempted to do so in such a way that they did not get a "habit" (become physically dependent) again. However, nearly all (39 out of 44) of respondents experienced withdrawal symptoms. Most described how they initially invested a great deal of effort to ensure a supply of opiates but were not able to maintain a continuous supply. Many prisoners experience recurring bouts of withdrawal symptoms as the following case study illustrates.

Dave, a 28 year old man, who was imprisoned for 18 months, described how he was "sick" (withdrawal from drugs) at different times throughout his imprisonment. He would find a source of money or heroin which would last for a limited period of time ending when the supply ran dry or he, or the prisoner supplying the heroin, was moved to another wing or prison. He would then experience withdrawal symptoms again until he found a new source of money or heroin.

The introduction of MDT in English and Welsh prisons is reported to have had a further effect on the frequency of drug use. Edgar found that 15% (n=17) of drug users in his study reduced the frequency of their drug use. Reductions in use were most common amongst cannabis users.

Are there changes in the types of drug used by prisoners?

The data presented earlier in this document suggest that while there are many different drugs available in prison the majority of prisoners use cannabis. Even those who may have been using drugs other than cannabis in the community do so when imprisoned.

Turnbull's qualitative study found that prisoners expressed a preference for cannabis, or for narcotics such as heroin, or tranquillisers such as benzodiazepines. Cannabis was often cited as "the best prison drug" while most said that they were less willing to use stimulants such as amphetamines. The lack of the means with which to buy or otherwise obtain opiates or benzodiazepines on a regular basis led many to make do with cannabis.

Imprisonment and exposure to Mandatory Drug Testing is believed to have an effect on the types of drugs prisoners use. Edgar and colleagues found 10% of those in their study had changed the drugs they used in some way. These prisoners had:

- altered their balance from cannabis to heroin (n=7 6%);

- experimented with heroin (n=4 4%).

Most of those who reported using less cannabis but using more heroin maintained it was a strategic response to the drug testing regime, as can be seen from the quote below.

> "Before MDT, I would have the foil (smoking heroin) maybe once a month and cannabis every day. Now I would have a draw (cannabis) once in a while but use the foil a couple of times a week. When I switched over, initially I was on it every day. Now it's down to a couple of times a week. The MDT has made me change over. I won't get detected as the gear is too poor quality. It might come up on the screening, but never on

confirmation. They know I'm using, but it is so little and such poor quality that they will never catch me." (Edgar et al 1998)

Those who used heroin for the first time in response to MDT (n=4) did not persist with heroin use, only using the drug on the odd occasion.

Such changes in drug use, Edgar speculates, appear to be dependent on a number of factors. Foremost was the calculation of risk of being selected for MDT, and then being detected, and the risk of punishment.

The types of drug used by prisoner are, to some extent, based on availability. Turnbull reports that most of the prisoners in his study (n=42) used at least two different drugs. The majority opportunistically using a mixture of drugs throughout their stay in prison. The picture that emerges from this study is one of a range of drugs regularly available, but where individual levels of drug use decrease and patterns of use alter. Drug shortages or "droughts" were mentioned but were never described as being extensive enough to significantly affect their overall level of use.

Route of administration

The most common way of taking drugs among imprisoned drugs users is smoking. The most commonly used drug is cannabis and the most common method of taking it is smoking.

However, there is some evidence that some people may be initiated into drug injection in prison. Gore and colleagues found that this was the case for a quarter of IDUs interviewed in HMP Glenochil and 6% of injectors in Barlinnie prison (Gore et al 1995) . In a study of drug transitions (the move from oral or inhalation to injecting), 7% of heroin users had their first experience of injecting while in prison (B.Powis, personal communication). Of 3 922 prisoners surveyed in 1997/98, 1% (41) reported having injected for the first time while in prison (Department of Health 1999).

While the data on initiation to injecting is still scanty, research has consistently shown the continued injection of drugs in prison by those injecting prior to imprisonment. The published research indicates that about a quarter to a third of drug injectors manage to inject at some time when they are in prison.

Many IDUs, therefore, stop injecting while in prison. Turnbull identifies a number of reasons for doing so which can be broadly grouped into:

- personal choice (including an assessment of the risks associated with injecting);

- practical (including the problems of acquiring drugs and needles and syringes);

- economic (the cost of drugs);

- stigmatisation (the attitudes of others);

- decreased overall drug consumption (absence of a '"habit").

The discontinuation of injecting is probably influenced by a combination of these factors.

Surveys have consistently shown the continued injection of drugs by a substantial minority of IDUs (see table 1). Turnbull found that those who continued to inject drugs in prison consisted of two main groups (Turnbull 1994). There were those who indicated that they always intended to continue to inject, and there were those who continued or resumed injecting due to circumstances and immediate influences. Many prisoners resolved not to inject drugs, but when needles and syringes became accessible they injected. The availability of drugs and injecting equipment appeared to be a dominant influence for continued injecting drug use.

Research in the United Kingdom indicates that those who continue to inject do at irregular intervals and at a reduced level, compared to injecting in the community prior to imprisonment. In a qualitative study IDUs reported a variety of patterns of injecting. Some were able to sustain daily injection of drugs. Those who were able to inject daily were imprisoned for a shorter period of time, often on remand, and were held in a prison in, or close to, their home town. However, most injected once a week or several times a month. The frequency of injecting ranged from one to 48 times with a mean of 17.9 injections over a 25-week period (Turnbull et al 1994).

Whilst many of those who inject in prison do so less frequently than when in the community outside of prisons, significant changes occur in the other aspects of their injecting behaviour. Currently there is no supply of clean injecting equipment in prisons in England and Wales as there is in the community. The majority of those who inject in prison do so with used equipment. As the data in table one shows those who inject in prison are likely to do so with previously used injecting equipment. Between 60 to 80% of those who inject in prison report sharing needles and syringes on at least one occasion.

Several studies have tracked changes in sharing behaviour of imprisoned IDUs. Turnbull describes the changes in the sharing behaviour of 164 IDUs before, during and after imprisonment (Turnbull et al 1991):

- before imprisonment 45 % of those injecting (n=164) shared syringes;

- during imprisonment 73% of those injecting (n=45) shared syringes;

- since release 63% of those injecting (n=103) shared syringes.

Table 1:   Drug injectors reporting injecting and sharing in prison

Location	Injecting when in prison		Sharing syringes in prison	
	%	n	%	n
England, Wales and Scotland (Dolan et al 1990)	23	139	75	32
England 1989/90 (Donoghoe et al 1992)	25	474	62	119
London/Bristol 1989/90 (Dolan et al 1991)	27	111	70	30
Wales 1990 (Keene et al 1993)	51	69	74	35
Glasgow 1990 (Covell et al 1993)	16	262	73	41
England 1990 (Turnbull et al 1991)	27	168	71	45
Scotland 1990 (Power et al 1992)	28	154	76	32
Scotland 1991 (Shewan et al 1994)	25	33	76	25
London 1993 (Turnbull et al 1994)	21	99	67	21
Glenochil 1993 (Taylor 1995)	43	76	100	32
England and Wales (1997)	47	485	80	229

(Department of Health 1999)

In a survey of nearly 4 000 inmates, 12% (n=485) reported injecting in the four weeks prior to imprisonment. Of this group 150 (31%) reported sharing needles and syringes at this time. While in prison, 47% (n=229) of those who were injecting on entry into prison continued to inject, of which the majority (80% n=184) shared needles and syringes.

Several other factors have been identified which potentially increase the risk from injecting drug use within the prison environment. Intermittent and impromptu injection of drugs means that it is usually unplanned. The immediate need to take drugs can sometimes mean that little attention is paid to how drugs are injected. Often, especially in the early stages of imprisonment, drugs are injected when users are experiencing withdrawal symptoms. Some IDUs in prison also have a very limited conception of sharing. For example, if there is a time-gap between episodes of the syringe's use, or if the person who had previously injected with the syringe was not actually present when it was used again, such sharing was described as "just using old works" and was not seen as risky (Turnbull et al 1996).

Imprisonment, therefore, for those who continue to inject often results in a increase in unsafe injecting practices carrying a higher risk of HIV and hepatitis infection.

The sharing of injecting equipment is not restricted to needles and syringes, but encompasses the sharing of spoons and other devices used for preparing drugs. Such injecting paraphernalia include filters through which the drug solutions is drawn, and the containers of water used to flush out injecting equipment. These practices have implications for the transmission of blood-borne viruses.

The sharing of cookers and filters is particularly common amongst those who inject in prison, and some as a means of sharing drugs routinely practices front- or back- loading. Prisoners have also mentioned sharing the residue of drugs left during the preparation, such as that which is left in the cooker or filter. Although such practices are engaged in outside of prison, they appear to be more common in prison because of the scarcity of resources (injecting paraphernalia and drugs). Furthermore such items are likely to be shared among a larger number of individuals within the prison environment, whereas in the community such sharing behaviour tends to occur between sexual partners and close friends.

Treatment

Until recently, only a handful of specialist units operated within prison providing intensive treatment for those with drug problems. The majority of drug using prisoners received little help or treatment from the prison service with some support being provided by community based services. Health care provision for drug users in prison is not equivalent to that available in the community. Substitute prescribing within prison is mainly the provision of symptomatic treatment or short term methadone detoxification. There is no provision for longer term maintenance prescribing. Drug using prisoners who were receiving treatment in the community prior to imprisonment are not able to continue with their treatment.

Treatment services for drug using prisoners are currently undergoing rapid development in English and Welsh prisons. The Prison Service has received £50 million to spend on drug treatment for prisoners during the next three years. Four main strands of services are planned: CARAT (Counselling, Assessment, Referral, Advice and Throughcare) services; detoxification; rehabilitation programmes; and therapeutic communities. Each prison will have a CARAT service designed to be a low level intervention identifying drug users, providing ongoing support and advice throughout their time in prison, referring them on to appropriate intensive intervention, and providing continuity between treatment in prison and that available on release. Thirty-five intensive detoxification programmes are to be established using new health care standards based on a clinical review of practice. A total of sixty rehabilitation programmes are to be provided in prisons by community based drug services. Finally, eight therapeutic communities are to be developed.

There are no plans to introduce drug maintenance programmes or needle exchanges (which are the most common types of service provided to drug users in the community).

Motivation to stop using

As pointed out earlier, many drug users stop using when imprisoned. Generally, this is because of the difficulties of sustaining drug use given the level of surveillance and the threat of possible detection, the difficulty in getting and maintaining a supply of drugs, a lack of resources to purchase drugs and the desire to use the opportunity to change their lifestyle and drug using behaviour.

Edgar and colleagues in their assessment of the effects of MDT on drug use amongst prison identified that one third of the drug users in their sample (37/111) were deterred from using drugs because of the threat of punishment for a positive test. For some, formal punishment constituted a powerful threat. Young offenders, in particular, reported that they had stopped using drugs because of the risk of additional days being added to their sentence. Other inmates attributed their change to "collateral effects of detection" such as the withdrawal of privileges (such as access to a gym, home leave) and the impact on relationships with their families. As mentioned earlier MDT appears to have had a greater impact on those were cannabis users (46% stopped using) than those who used heroin (13% stopped using).

Turnbull reports that some prisoners attempt to use prison as a place to stop using drugs, or at least have a rest from the type of drug use and lifestyle they had outside of prison, as can be seen from the quotes below.

"Prisons are the best detox in the world – two weeks and you're off." (27 year old male, imprisoned for six months)

"I felt like I had to use the time in prison as a rest from drugs, it's good to use the time to recuperate." (33 year old male, held in a central London prison)

However, for others who set out to use their time constructively in prison their endeavours were far from successful. Many reported the availability of drugs combined with the lack of support made abstinence difficult.

"I think deep down inside I wanted to get off them [drugs]... but in that situation, in that environment... I knew I couldn't do it on my own... even though I wanted to deep inside."

In a qualitative study of IDUs recently released from prisons in England and Wales, respondents gave substantial reasons for their continued use of drugs (Turnbull et al, 1994). Some saw drug use as a natural and fundamental behaviour for them, and most thought of it as unavoidable and necessary in prison. This was particularly the case in the first few weeks or months of imprisonment, when drugs were needed to alleviate the withdrawal symptoms or longer term insomnia resulting from the cessation of opiate use. These respondents thought their drug use was justified because when withdrawing from opiates, the insomnia and other symptoms they suffered made them feel as if they were "doing double time". Even those who do not refer to their drug use as a direct consequence of withdrawing from opiates see their drug use as necessary to help them get to sleep. The causes of insomnia most commonly cited in this context were anxiety, depression, boredom and physical inactivity.

Summary and conclusions

The effect of imprisonment on drug use appears to be considerable. Some of the effects can be regarded as positive (stopping and reducing drug use, fewer drug users injecting drugs and treatment). Other effects are negative (switching to more harmful drug use patterns, sharing injecting equipment, the risk of viral transmission).

There is strong evidence that drug use in prison is common. Cannabis appears to be widely used, and the use of other drugs is prevalent among some groups (mainly those who were using them prior to imprisonment). Even so, studies show that the amount and range of drugs used in prison are less than is the case in the community. As Shewan and colleagues have noted, prison is a modifier of people's drug use (Shewan et al, 1994). It seems safe to assume that for the most part many of those who used drugs prior to imprisonment at least reduce, if not stop, using. Prison is an environment in which drugs are available, but one in which people's levels of drug use decrease. For a significant minority (between 20% and 30%) prison appears to be a place where they stop using drugs.

It is important to recognise that patterns of drug use do vary between different groups in the prison population. Many of those who were casual or recreational users in the community appear to rarely use drugs when imprisoned. Those who had more dependent use in the community are more likely to continue using in prison. This group are also more likely to use a range of different drugs. However, most prisoners who used drugs in the community appear to use less frequently and in smaller quantities. Some prisoners use any drug that is available. Only a minority appear to change from the use of less harmful drugs to more harmful drugs.

The majority of prisoners smoke their drugs. Many of those who inject drugs in the community stop injecting when imprisoned and move to other routes of administration. A significant minority continue to inject however. While many of

143

those who inject do so on fewer occasions, they are more likely to do so with previously used injecting equipment when compared with their injecting behaviour prior to imprisonment. Other injecting paraphernalia is generally re-used and shared also. The risk of transmission of HIV and other blood-borne viruses among those who share needles and syringes and other injecting paraphernalia is of major concern.

The effect of prison based treatment on drug use within prison has not been assessed to date (although a follow-up study of those who received treatment in prison-based treatment services is due to report soon). Given the lack of treatment provision, until recently, it seems reasonable to suggest that any effect has been minimal. Indeed the lack of detoxification facilities and other treatment services may have encouraged continuation of drug use for those prisoners who are more heavily dependent. However, the considerable new investment in prison drug services should, in time, pay dividends.

MDT appears to have an impact on the motivation of some prisoners to stop using drug. The impact appears to be greatest with young, cannabis users rather than long-term heroin users. For some of those who continue to use drugs they report that this is because of the lack of adequate treatment. Others report that they continue to use drugs because of insomnia, boredom, depression and physical inactivity.

Appendix

Drug Use by Prisoners – Guidelines

Richard Muscat

Background

Following the approval of the Permanent Correspondents at their 40th meeting in October 1997, two meetings took place, one in Lisbon in July 1998 and the other at the first Project Group Meeting in the field of Epidemiology (30 November-1 December 1998). The first working group meeting was held in Paris on the 26 March 1999, a report of which was forwarded to all interested parties by Ms. Luisa Machado Rodrigues. The major outcome of that meeting was that a key list of words or guidelines be provided to each member by the co-ordinator for discussion at the second working group meeting in June. The basis for such a document will then provide a template for a country/city report to form part of the general literature review of the area of drug use in prisons. The literature review in turn needs to be completed by the co-ordinator by the end of September at the latest and should aim to provide a country/city profile of drug use in prison. This task may be aided and abetted by the use of a map/s as is the case in the ESPAD study and now the Multi-city Study which should facilitate presentation of the findings.

Current Studies in the Field

It is imperative to take into account the current work being undertaken in most European countries in relation to drug use in prison. The following organisations to some extent, whether by accident or default, have data on particular aspects of the problem in relation to their own particular interests.

1. *European Network on HIV/Aids and Hepatitis Prevention in Prison*

HIV and Hepatitis prevalence and related risk behaviours amongst prisoners that include drug use amongst others. Methodology is well implemented and validated. Data include number of prisons in each of the countries, number of prisoners, %female, %remand, %non-resident, drug substitution programmes, needle exchange, proportion of IDUs in the prison population.

2. *European Network of Drug and HIV/Aids Services in Prison*

1994/1995 general estimates of the proportion of prisoners who were problematic drug users. Responses were in the range of 30-50%. In 1998, 3 000 questionnaires distributed, returns 189, with the result that 46.3% were estimated to be users of illegal drugs before incarceration.

145

3.   *EMCDDA* country reports, however countries report different aspects pertaining to the problem.

4.   *Council of Europe* Annual Penal Statistics (SPACE)

Part 1 concerns prison populations and prison staff and Part 2 non-custodial measures and sanctions. There were some problems with missing data and inconsistencies within a particular item or between two different items.

5.   *Council of Europe, Human Rights Division, European Committee for the Prevention of Torture and Inhuman or Degrading Treatment or Punishment (CPT).* Data related to testing in prison.

6.   *Council of Europe, Pompidou Group.* Multicity Study, NCT-13 Convictions for drug law offences. Treatment Demand Study, Table F2, Type of Treatment Centre.

7.   *European Commission PHARE* Project: Harm Reduction in Prison.

Literature pertaining to what needs to be done in this sector:

1.   *WHO and UNAIDS.* Recommendations,

2.   International Self-Report Delinquency Study.

Data related to drug use and criminal offences in the 14-21 age cohort.

We have also been asked to contribute our review to the documents needed for the forthcoming seminar in October 1999 on "Drug Misusing Offenders in Prison and After Release" organised by the Pompidou Group.

With all these considerations in mind the following suggested format is being put forward for your appraisal. It is envisaged that such a document will allow for the collection of country/city data that will give us some insight into the nature of the problem in each country/city and what might be appropriate for the next phase that is instrument development.

Drug Use by Prisoners
Country/City data form

Name:
Country:
Year/month: (see 3 below)
e-mail:
FAX:

1. Inclusion Criteria:

Prison/s
All confined individuals
Those confined and awaiting sentence
Those confined in special Prison facilities

2. Exclusion Criteria:

Those presently at centres outside the prison confines
Probationers
House arrest, day reporting, community based programmes

3. The data submitted in the following pertains to a particular year or month

Section 1: basic information

1. Total number of prison/s

2. Total number of inmates

3. Total number of non-citizens

4. a. Total number of sentenced inmates
   b. Total number of inmates awaiting sentence

5. a Adult males aged 18 or over
   b. Median age
   c. Adult females aged 18 or over
   d. Median age
   e. Juvenile males aged under 18
   f. Juvenile females aged under 18

6. Highest educational level completed of all inmates
   a. never went to school/never completed primary school
   b. primary school
   c. secondary school

d.   Tertiary education
e.   Not known

Section 2: Drug Offences

7.   Total number of inmates sentenced for drug law offences

8.   Total number for each type of offence

Drug trafficking, possession, consumption, other

Adult male over 18
Adult female over 18
Juvenile male under 18
Juvenile female under 18

9.   Total number for type of drug involved with each drug offence

a.   Drug trafficking

Heroin, cocaine, amphetamine, ecstasy, cannabis, other

Adult male over 18
Adult female over 18
Juvenile male under 18
Juvenile female under 18

b.   Possession.

Heroin, cocaine, amphetamine ecstasy, cannabis, other

Adult male over 18
Adult female over 18
Juvenile male under 18
Juvenile female under 18

c.   Consumption

Heroin, cocaine, amphetamine, ecstasy, cannabis, other

Adult male over 18
Adult female over 18
Juvenile male under 18
Juvenile female under 18

d.   Other

   Heroin, cocaine amphetamine, ecstasy, cannabis, other

Adult male over 18
Adult female over 18
Juvenile male under 18
Juvenile female under 18

10.   Sentence length for each drug offence

a.   Trafficking

   <1m, 1-3, 4-6, 7-12, 13-36, 37-60, 61-120, 121-240, 240+, life

Adult male over 18
Adult female over 18
Juvenile male under 18
Juvenile female under 18

b.   Possession

   <1m, 1-3, 4-6, 7-12, 13-36, 37-60, 61-120, 121-240, 240+, life

Adult male over 18
Adult female over 18
Juvenile male under18
Juvenile female under 18

c.   Consumption

   <1m, 1-3, 4-6, 7-12, 13-36, 37-60, 61-120,121-240, 240+, life

Adult male over 18
Adult female over 18
Juvenile male under 18
Juvenile female under 18

d.   Other

   <1m, 1-3, 4-6, 7-12, 13-36, 37-60, 61-120, 121-240, 240+,life

Adult male over 18
Adult female over 18
Juvenile male under 18
Juvenile female under 18

11. For all Drug law offences - number of repeating offenders.

1st Offence, 2nd, 3rd, 4th, 5th 6th

Adult male over 18
Adult female over 18
Juvenile male under 18
Juvenile female under 18

12. Number of inmates with a previous history of drug use for all offences.

Drug law offences   Non-drug law offences

Adult male over 18
Adult female over 18
Juvenile male under 18
Juvenile female under 18

13. Previous employment of all inmates sentenced for drug law offences.

Employed, employed part time, unemployed, unknown

Adult male over 18
Adult female over 18
Juvenile male under 18
Juvenile female under 18

14. Educational level of all inmates sentenced for drug law offences

No schooling, primary, secondary, tertiary, unknown

Adult male over 18
Adult female over 18
Juvenile male under 18
Juvenile female under 18

Section 3: Health

15. Health status of inmates sentenced for drug law offences and non-drug law offences

    a.   Drug law offences

Aids, HIV, Hep C, TB

Adult male over 18

Adult female over 18
Juvenile male under 18
Juvenile female under 18

b.   Non-drug law offences.

Aids, HIV, Hep C, TB

Adult male over 18
Adult female over 18
Juvenile male under 18
Juvenile female under 18

16. Mental health status of inmates sentenced for drug law offences and non-drug offences

a.   Drug Law Offences

24 hour mental health care, mental health therapy

Adult male over 18
Adult female over 18
Juvenile male under 18
Juvenile female under 18

b.   Non-drug law offences

24 hour mental health care, mental health therapy

Adult male over 18
Adult female over 18
Juvenile male under 18
Juvenile female under 18

17. Number of inmates sentenced for drug law offences and non-drug law offences receiving psychotropic medication

Drug law offences   Non-drug law offences

Adult male over 18
Adult female over 18
Juvenile male under 18
Juvenile female under 18

18. Number of inmates in drug treatment who committed drug law offences and non-drug law offences

Drug law offence   Non-drug law offences

Adult male over 18
Adult female over 18
Juvenile male under 18
Juvenile female under 18

19. Number of inmates in type of treatment provided for drug law offenders and non drug law offenders

    a.   Drug law offenders

            *Detox, I. Couns. G. Couns. Subs, Methad Maint, Abs, Other
       Adult male over 18
       Adult female over 18
       Juvenile male under 18
       Juvenile female under 18

    b.   Non-drug law offenders

            *Detox, I. Couns. G.Couns. Subs. Methad Maint. Abs. Other

       Adult male over 18
       Adult female over 18
       Juvenile male under 18
       Juvenile female under 18

*(Detox. = Detoxification; I. Couns. = Individual counselling; G. Couns. = Group Counselling; Subs. = Substitution therapy; Methad Maint = Methadone Maintenance; Abs. = Abstinence).

Section 4: Drug testing in prison

20. a.   Drug testing on entry: Yes   No

    b.   Type of test: written…………interview…………urine test…………

    c.   Number of positive tests of inmates sentenced for drug law offences.

            Heroin, Cocaine, Amphet, Ecstasy, Cannabis, other

       Adult male over 18
       Adult female over 18
       Juvenile males under 18
       Juvenile female under 18

d. Number of positive tests of inmates sentenced for non-drug law offences

Heroin, Cocaine, Amphet, Ecstasy, Cannabis, Other

Adult male over 18
Adult female over 18
Juvenile male under 18
Juvenile female under 18

21. a. Mandatory Drug Testing   Yes   No

b. Type of test: written.............interview...........urine test

c. Frequency of test...............

d. Which category of inmate is tested under this format.................

e. Number of inmates in this category...............

f. Number positive tests for inmates described in d.

Heroin, Cocaine, Amphet, Ecstasy, Cannabis, Other

Adult male over 18
Adult female over 18
Juvenile male under 18
Juvenile female under 18

22. a. Random Drug Testing   Yes   No

b. Type of test: written............interview...........urine test..............

c. Frequency of test...............

d. Which category of inmate is tested under this format....................

e. Number of inmates in this category....................

f. Number of positive tests for inmates described in d.

Heroin, Cocaine, Amphet, Ecstasy, Cannabis, Other.

Adult male over 18
Adult female over 18
Juvenile male under 18
Juvenile female under 18

Section 5: After care

23. Are there any services available for the drug user on release from prison:
Yes   No

24. If Yes, what type are available?

    a.   Help with social integration......
    b.   Contacts with care services......
    c.   Relapse prevention......
    d.   Other......

25. What is the number of drug users making use of such services........................

26. Of these using such services and those that do not how many of each category end up in prison within one year of release.

Number back in Prison:

                                          Service user   Non user

        Adult male over 18
        Adult female over 18
        Juvenile male under 18
        Juvenile female under 18

Notes:

Section 1: most of this information may be obtained from SPACE (Council of Europe) for those countries participating in the Council of Europe's study on the collection of criminal justice data.

Section 2: As in section 1 data may be obtained from SPACE in addition to the Multicity Study organised by the Pompidou Group.

Section 3: Most of data here can be found to some extent from the European Network on Aids/HIV prevention in prisons and the Network of Drug and HIV/AIDS services in prison and the Treatment Demand reporting system of the Pompidou Group.

Section 4: The Council of Europe, Human Rights Division, European Committee for the Prevention of Torture and Inhuman or Degrading Treatment or Punishment (CPT) group, of the Human Rights Division of the Council of Europe apparently have a data base (April launch date) of the drug testing abilities of a number of prisons within Europe.

Section 5: No known sources of information but possibly the network for drug and Aids/HIV services in prison might be of help.

It will also be helpful if each of the participants could submit an abstract with title, authors names and journal of the work published by that country/city in relation to drug use in prison. Literature that does not appear in scientific journals is also welcome as in the first working group meeting it was pointed out that some studies are carried out by the University and different groups that for one reason or another do not appear as such in the published literature.

7 May 1999
Richard Muscat

Sales agents for publications of the Council of Europe
Agents de vente des publications du Conseil de l'Europe

AUSTRALIA/AUSTRALIE
Hunter Publications, 58A, Gipps Street
AUS-3066 COLLINGWOOD, Victoria
Tel.: (61) 3 9417 5361
Fax: (61) 3 9419 7154
E-mail: Sales@hunter-pubs.com.au
http://www.hunter-pubs.com.au

AUSTRIA/AUTRICHE
Gerold und Co., Graben 31
A-1011 WIEN 1
Tel.: (43) 1 533 5014
Fax: (43) 1 533 5014 18
E-mail: buch@gerold.telecom.at
http://www.gerold.at

BELGIUM/BELGIQUE
La Librairie européenne SA
50, avenue A. Jonnart
B-1200 BRUXELLES 20
Tel.: (32) 2 734 0281
Fax: (32) 2 735 0860
E-mail: info@libeurop.be
http://www.libeurop.be

Jean de Lannoy
202, avenue du Roi
B-1190 BRUXELLES
Tel.: (32) 2 538 4308
Fax: (32) 2 538 0841
E-mail: jean.de.lannoy@euronet.be
http://www.jean-de-lannoy.be

CANADA
Renouf Publishing Company Limited
5369 Chemin Canotek Road
CDN-OTTAWA, Ontario, K1J 9J3
Tel.: (1) 613 745 2665
Fax: (1) 613 745 7660
E-mail: order.dept@renoufbooks.com
http://www.renoufbooks.com

CZECH REPUBLIC/
RÉPUBLIQUE TCHÈQUE
USIS, Publication Service
Havelkova 22
CZ-130 00 PRAHA 3
Tel./Fax: (420) 2 2423 1114

DENMARK/DANEMARK
Munksgaard
35 Norre Sogade, PO Box 173
DK-1005 KØBENHAVN K
Tel.: (45) 7 733 3333
Fax: (45) 7 733 3377
E-mail: direct@munksgaarddirect.dk
http://www.munksgaarddirect.dk

FINLAND/FINLANDE
Akateeminen Kirjakauppa
Keskuskatu 1, PO Box 218
FIN-00381 HELSINKI
Tel.: (358) 9 121 41
Fax: (358) 9 121 4450
E-mail: akatilaus@stockmann.fi
http://www.akatilaus.akateeminen.com

GERMANY/ALLEMAGNE
UNO Verlag
Proppelsdorfer Allee 55
D-53115 BONN
Tel.: (49) 2 28 94 90 231
Fax: (49) 2 28 21 74 92
E-mail: unoverlag@aol.com
http://www.uno-verlag.de

GREECE/GRÈCE
Librairie Kauffmann
Mavrokordatou 9
GR-ATHINAI 106 78
Tel.: (30) 1 38 29 283
Fax: (30) 1 38 33 967

HUNGARY/HONGRIE
Euro Info Service
Hungexpo Europa Kozpont ter 1
H-1101 BUDAPEST
Tel.: (361) 264 8270
Fax: (361) 264 8271
E-mail: euroinfo@euroinfo.hu
http://www.euroinfo.hu

ITALY/ITALIE
Libreria Commissionaria Sansoni
Via Duca di Calabria 1/1, CP 552
I-50125 FIRENZE
Tel.: (39) 556 4831
Fax: (39) 556 41257
E-mail: licosa@licosa.com
http://www.licosa.com

NETHERLANDS/PAYS-BAS
De Lindeboom Internationale Publikaties
PO Box 202, MA de Ruyterstraat 20 A
NL-7480 AE HAAKSBERGEN
Tel.: (31) 53 574 0004
Fax: (31) 53 572 9296
E-mail: lindeboo@worldonline.nl
http://home-1-worldonline.nl/~lindeboo/

NORWAY/NORVÈGE
Akademika, A/S Universitetsbokhandel
PO Box 84, Blindern
N-0314 OSLO
Tel.: (47) 22 85 30 30
Fax: (47) 23 12 24 20

POLAND/POLOGNE
Głowna Księgarnia Naukowa
im. B. Prusa
Krakowskie Przedmiescie 7
PL-00-068 WARSZAWA
Tel.: (48) 29 22 66
Fax: (48) 22 26 64 49
E-mail: inter@internews.com.pl
http://www.internews.com.pl

PORTUGAL
Livraria Portugal
Rua do Carmo, 70
P-1200 LISBOA
Tel.: (351) 13 47 49 82
Fax: (351) 13 47 02 64
E-mail: liv.portugal@mail.telepac.pt

SPAIN/ESPAGNE
Mundi-Prensa Libros SA
Castelló 37
E-28001 MADRID
Tel.: (34) 914 36 37 00
Fax: (34) 915 75 39 98
E-mail: libreria@mundiprensa.es
http://www.mundiprensa.com

SWITZERLAND/SUISSE
BERSY
Route d'Uvrier 15
CH-1958 LIVRIER/SION
Tel.: (41) 27 203 73 30
Fax: (41) 27 203 73 32
E-mail: bersy@freesurf.ch

UNITED KINGDOM/ROYAUME-UNI
TSO (formerly HMSO)
51 Nine Elms Lane
GB-LONDON SW8 5DR
Tel.: (44) 207 873 8372
Fax: (44) 207 873 8200
E-mail: customer.services@theso.co.uk
http://www.the-stationery-office.co.uk
http://www.itsofficial.net

UNITED STATES and CANADA/
ÉTATS-UNIS et CANADA
Manhattan Publishing Company
468 Albany Post Road, PO Box 850
CROTON-ON-HUDSON,
NY 10520, USA
Tel.: (1) 914 271 5194
Fax: (1) 914 271 5856
E-mail: Info@manhattanpublishing.com
http://www.manhattanpublishing.com

STRASBOURG
Librairie Kléber
Palais de l'Europe
F-67075 STRASBOURG Cedex
Fax: (33) 03 88 52 91 21

Council of Europe Publishing/Editions du Conseil de l'Europe
F-67075 Strasbourg Cedex
Tel.: (33) 03 88 41 25 81 – Fax: (33) 03 88 41 39 10
E-mail: publishing@coe.int – Web site: http://book.coe.int